Die FehlerHilfe

Das Aktiv-Training gegen typische Fehler

Englisch

Grammatik 7.–9. Schuljahr

Schroedel

Die FehlerHilfe

Englisch Grammatik
7. bis 9. Schuljahr

Autorin:
Sarah Nowotny stammt aus London und verfügt über langjährige Erfahrung als Englisch-Lehrerin. Außerdem arbeitet sie als freie Autorin und Übersetzerin.

Druck 2 / Jahr 2011

Redaktion: Dr. Christine Steinhoff
Kontakt: lernhilfen@schroedel.de
Herstellung: Sandra Grünberg
Umschlaggestaltung und Innenlayout: tiff.any GmbH, Berlin
Illustrationen: Thies Schwarz, Hannover
Satz: imprint, Zusmarshausen
Druck und Bindung: westermann druck GmbH, Braunschweig

ISBN: 978-3-507-**23205**-1

Inhaltsverzeichnis

Vorwort

Liebe Schülerin, lieber Schüler,

du möchtest weniger Fehler machen und deine Noten verbessern?
Dann ist **Die FehlerHilfe** genau das Richtige für dich! **Die FehlerHilfe** hilft dir, typische Fehler zu vermeiden und so deine Leistungen zu steigern.

Zu jedem wichtigen Thema gibt es ein Kapitel. Jedes Kapitel beginnt mit einem Auszug aus einer Klassenarbeit. Hier siehst du, welche Fehler häufig gemacht werden. Sind in deiner Klassenarbeit ähnliche Fehler angestrichen? Dann solltest du dieses Kapitel auf jeden Fall bearbeiten!

Die Kapitel bestehen aus folgenden Bausteinen:

Regeln	Hier wird leicht verständlich erklärt, welche Regeln du beachten musst, um typische Fehler zu vermeiden.
Übungen	Mithilfe der Übungen kannst du die Regeln aktiv trainieren.
Tipps	Eingestreute Tipps geben dir zusätzliche Hilfestellungen.
Fehler-Check	Am Ende des Kapitels kannst du den Test machen: Alles fehlerfrei?

Die **Lösungen** zu den Übungen und zum Fehler-Check findest du am Ende des Buches.

Und nun kannst du dem Fehlerteufel den Kampf ansagen!

Viel Erfolg wünscht dir
Sarah Nowotny

Zeitformen (*tenses*) richtig gebrauchen

Present perfect oder *simple past*?

I was never in London, but last year I have visited Dover on the south II
coast of England. I have stayed with my aunt who lived there for three II
years so far. She loves it there! In fact, she has moved to a new house I
last week, but I didn't go there yet. Last summer, when I have been II
there, she has taken me to lots of different places, even to the beach! I
Unfortunately the water has been too cold to swim. I

Regeln

Present perfect und *simple past* benutzt man, um über die **Vergangenheit** zu sprechen. Aber wann verwendet man das eine und wann das andere? Das ist gar nicht so einfach zu entscheiden, weil diese beiden Zeitformen etwas anders funktionieren als im Deutschen. Es gibt jedoch einige Hinweise, die dir beim richtigen Gebrauch des *simple past* und des *present perfect* helfen.

1. Das ***simple past*** benutzt du für Ereignisse und Handlungen, die abgeschlossen sind. Es wird oft zusammen mit genauen Zeitangaben verwendet. Signalwörter sind zum Beispiel:
   yesterday, last week, in 2009, a month ago, when (I was ten)
   Beispiele: *I saw "Avatar" last Thursday with Jack and Louise.*
   We ate at a fantastic restaurant when we were in London.

2. Das ***present perfect*** verwendest du, um über Ereignisse oder Handlungen zu sprechen, die schon passiert sind, aber Auswirkungen auf die Gegenwart haben.
   Beispiele: *Oh no! I've lost my mobile!* (Ich habe mein Handy verloren, mit der Folge, dass ich jetzt niemanden anrufen kann.)
   Sorry, I haven't tidied up my room yet. (Ich habe mein Zimmer noch nicht aufgeräumt, sodass es immer noch unordentlich ist.)

3. Das ***present perfect*** benutzt du außerdem für Handlungen oder Ereignisse, die unmittelbar zuvor stattgefunden haben. Das Signalwort lautet hier: ***just***.
Beispiele: *She has just got an e-mail from Mike.*
Thank you, but I've just had lunch.

4. Weitere wichtige Signalwörter für das ***present perfect*** sind: *ever, never, already, yet, so far, lately, recently.*
Beispiele: *Have you ever been to the U.S.?*
Tim has already broken his leg twice.

Übungen

1 Choose the correct alternative in the following sentences.

a) Tom has gone/went on holiday yesterday. He'll be back next week.
b) Christopher Columbus has discovered/discovered the American continent in 1492.
c) I didn't eat/haven't eaten all day, so now I'm really hungry.
d) "Would you like something to drink?"
"No thanks. I've just had/I just had a can of Coke."
e) I haven't finished/didn't finish my essay yet, so I should really stay in this evening and do it.
f) We forgot/have forgotten to invite Lisa to the party, but if we phone her now she might still be able to come.
g) My uncle moved to Australia when I was two years old, and that was the last time I saw/have seen him.
h) Have you ever tried/Did you ever try inline skating? It's good fun!
i) I've tried/I tried water-skiing in Greece last year. It was quite tricky!
j) I think someone stole/has stolen my bike! I can't find it anywhere!

2 Choose a verb from the list below and put it into the correct sentence in the correct form.

catch ▪ break ▪ do ▪ leave ▪ live ▪ lose ▪ meet ▪ miss ▪ move ▪ pass ▪ see ▪ shave ▪ win

a) Fiona ______________________ all her exams so far this year.

b) ________ you ever __________ a competition?

c) My parents _________ here in 1998 and _______________ in the same house ever since.

d) I _____________ my homework, so I can spend the rest of the evening watching TV!

e) "________ you ________ Alan lately?"
"Yes, I _________ him in town last week. He says hello!"

f) How many times _______ Patrick _________ the maths lesson this week? He's going to get into trouble!

g) Mr O'Connor __________________ off his beard. He looks completely different now!

h) "Is Jack still there?"
"No, he ____________ about 10 minutes ago."

i) Helen ________________ her arm so she can't play volleyball for the next six weeks.

j) Our ice-hockey team _____________ our last game, so we need to do better the next time.

k) I have to stay in bed today. I _____________________ a cold.

3 Read the following sentences and correct any tenses that are wrong.

a) *I haven't seen Joanne at the party last night.*	
b) *I've just baked a cake for my mum – it's her birthday today.*	
c) *We didn't take the exam yet – it's not until next week.*	
d) *While Cindy was studying in the USA last year, she has kept in touch with her family via Skype.*	
e) *Did you already finish tidying your room? That was quick!*	
f) *I'm sorry, but I'm afraid I've forgotten your name. Who are you?*	
g) *"What time has Bill left?" "At 9 o'clock this morning."*	
h) *Jamie's posted some pictures of our holiday on Facebook, so you can see what a great time we had!*	
i) *I was here since 4 o'clock waiting for you! Why are you so late?*	
j) *This book has been written in 1890, but it's still interesting to read today.*	

4 Choose the correct alternative from the underlined words to complete the sentences below.

a) "My sister's already/just/since had a baby!" "Please give her my love!"
b) Frank arrived at 10 o'clock last night/next Monday/this week.
c) Have you prepared your presentation so far/yet/now?
d) Tim left school for three years/next month/in 2008.
e) Most people have never/ever/yet won any money in the lottery.
f) Five hundred years before/ago/then this region was just one big forest.
g) I've yet/already/this morning handed in my essay, so it's too late to change anything now.
h) How many texts have you sent so far/recently/ever this week?
i) They've been in contact through an internet chatroom for several months now, but they've already/often/never met in person.
j) My alarm clock rang at half-past six ago/this morning/lately.
k) Have you ever/already/just been to a rock festival?
l) I haven't spent so much time on my social networking pages recently/ever/yesterday, and I find I don't really miss it.
m) For two months/Just two months/Two months ago nobody knew his name; now he's famous!

Fehler-Check

Fill the gaps with the correct form of the verb in brackets.

When Jana Müller's parents first __________ (tell) her they were moving to Australia for three years, she ______________________ (not know) whether to be happy or sad. That _____________ (be) six months ago, and since then Jana ________________ (adapt) to life "down under" and ____________________(learn) to love the Aussie way of life.

"I ______________________(already/make) lots of new friends. So far I __________________ (visit) two of the great cities, Sydney and Melbourne, although we ______________ (not have) time to go to Adelaide yet. And my parents _________________ (book) a trip to the Great Barrier Reef for this year – I can't wait!"

At first Jana _____________ (not speak) the language very well, but her English ______________ (now/improve) and she _________________ (even/start) to speak with an Australian accent! And what does she miss most about Germany? "Real pretzels! But I ______________________ (just/discover) a shop near here run by a German couple who ________ (come) to live here in 1990 and who bake traditional German bread. The taste reminds me of home!"

☐ **Fehler**	**0 – 3 Fehler** **Super!**	**4 – 6 Fehler** **In Ordnung!**	**mehr als 6 Fehler** **Bitte noch einmal üben!**

Present perfect progressive

In our youth club this month we plan our new clubhouse. All this week **I**
we are decorating the rooms. I painted today which is why my clothes **II**
are so dirty, but it doesn't matter – I have only wear old clothes to do **I**
this work! But some people didn't help us at all today. Instead, they sat **II**
around – I hate lazy people like that!

Regeln

Neben dem *simple present perfect* gibt es auch eine *progressive*-Form (Verlaufsform) des *present perfect*. Um das *present perfect progressive* richtig zu bilden und zu verwenden, musst du dir folgende Regeln merken:

1. Das *present perfect progressive* setzt sich aus folgenden Bausteinen zusammen: *has/have + been + verb + –ing*.
   Beispiele: *They've been spending too much time on the computer.*
   He's been going to our school since January.

2. Von damals bis jetzt: Das *present perfect progressive* benutzt du, um über Handlungen oder Ereignisse zu sprechen, die in der Vergangenheit begonnen haben und in der Gegenwart noch andauern.
   Beispiele: *I've been studying very hard (and am still studying).*
   We've been getting things ready for Tony's party this evening (and are still getting things ready).

3. Wie beim *present perfect simple*, darfst du das *present perfect progressive* nicht benutzen, wenn du über einen **abgeschlossenen Zeitraum in der Vergangenheit** sprichst:
   Beispiele: *WRONG: ~~I've been feeding~~ my neighbour's cat last week while she was on holiday.*
   RIGHT: I fed my neighbour's cat last week while she was on holiday.

4. Das *present perfect progressive* benutzt du, um auszudrücken, **wie lange** eine bestimmte Aktivität schon andauert (von einem Punkt in der Vergangenheit bis jetzt). Wenn du dagegen ausdrücken willst, **wie oft** etwas schon geschehen ist, brauchst du eine *simple*-Form.
Beispiele: *WRONG: I'~~ve been playing~~ rugby four times this week.*
RIGHT: I've played rugby four times this week.

Übungen

1 Complete the sentences with one of the verbs below. Use the present perfect progressive.

cut ▪ do ▪ feel ▪ read ▪ run ▪ save ▪ search ▪ snow ▪ travel

a) The children ______________________ around all afternoon, so they must be tired now.

b) I ______________________ for the information I need on the Internet, but I haven't found it yet.

c) This term we ______________________ Shakespeare's "Macbeth" in our English class. It isn't always easy to understand!

d) "Why are you crying?" "I______________________ onions!"

e) It ______________________ for several hours now and the roads are very slippery, so please drive carefully!

f) Holly ______________________ her pocket money to buy tickets to the Pink concert.

g) I ______________________ sick all day. I think I'll go to bed early.

h) My cousin ______________________ around South America for the past three months, but he's coming home next week.

i) "What ______ you ______________ today?" "Oh, nothing much."

2 Change the sentences below. Use the present perfect progressive.

a) Gracie came to stay with us last Friday. She's still here now.

Gracie ______________________________ with us since last Friday.

b) I started to read a good book yesterday, but I haven't finished it yet.

I ___________________________ a good book this week.

c) We switched on the radio two hours ago and are still listening to it now. We ___________________________________ to the radio for two hours.

d) The sun was shining this morning and it's still sunny now.

The sun ____________________________ all day.

e) The children went swimming after lunch and haven't come back yet.

They ____________________________ since lunchtime.

f) My foot started to hurt after I fell over and it still hurts now.

My foot ____________________________ since I fell over.

3 Which alternative is correct?

a) How often have you been listening / have you listened to that CD?

b) How long have you been playing / have you played the guitar? You're really good!

c) I've been leaving / I've left a message for Tina three times this week, but she hasn't answered me yet.

d) How often has he been asking / has he asked you to dance?

e) She has been drinking / has drunk coffee all afternoon – she won't be able to sleep tonight!

Fehler-Check

Fill the gaps in the text below.
Use the words in brackets in the correct form.

Now we go live to Matt Shea for his report on the German team.

"The Germans ____________________ (train) hard all year and are ready for the challenge of this championship.

The team ____________________ (play) well so far but the players know that the next match won't be easy. They ____________________ (stay) at the hotel behind me since last Friday and ____________________ (relax) today after their match against Serbia. I asked their new captain what he ______________________ (do) since then.

'Not much, really! I _________________________ (watch) a bit of TV and ______________ (listen) to my MP3 player. Some of the other players ______________________ (work out) in the gym, and others ______________________ (phone) friends and family back home.

We ________________________ (look) at some videos of the next team we have to play against, too.' The team's coach, with the help of his assistants, __________________________ (do) all he can to make sure that the team is motivated for the next match. So let's wish them good luck and say: go Germany!"

☐ **Fehler**	**0 – 2 Fehler** Super!	**3 – 5 Fehler** In Ordnung!	**mehr als 5 Fehler** Bitte noch einmal üben!

Past perfect

Last year my father went back to visit his home town, for the first time
in 30 years. He found that many things changed. The park where he I
played with his friends was a shopping centre, and they painted lots of II
pictures onto the walls of his old school. He has lived in a very quiet I
street, which was now very busy – that had been the biggest surprise I
for him.

Regeln

Wie kannst du ausdrücken, dass eine Handlung in der Vergangenheit **vor** einer anderen Handlung in der Vergangenheit stattgefunden hat? Ganz einfach: Du nimmst das *past perfect*! Mit dem *past perfect* kannst du über die „Vergangenheit in der Vergangenheit" berichten. Die folgenden Regeln zeigen dir, wie diese Zeitform einzusetzen ist.

1. Um das *past perfect* zu bilden, brauchst du:
   had + past participle-Form des Verbs
   Beispiele: *The children felt sick because they had eaten too much.*
   She failed the test because she hadn't done enough work.

2. Du benutzt das *past perfect*, wenn du über zwei Ereignisse in der Vergangenheit reden willst, von denen eines vor dem anderen passiert ist. Nimm das *past perfect* für das zeitlich vorangegangene (erste) Ereignis und das *simple past* für das in der Vergangenheit nachfolgende (zweite).
   Beispiele: *Jerry couldn't play football because he had broken his leg.*
   We wanted to go to the new Twilight film, but Rob had already seen it.

Tipp | *When, after* oder *by the time* können dir signalisieren, dass du das *past perfect* brauchst.
Beispiele: *My brother had left the house by the time I got up.*

Übungen

1 Complete the sentences using the past perfect.
Make sure the verb form is correct!

a) By the time we got to the party, they _______________ (drink) all the lemonade.

b) Charlie was very tired because he _______________ (not/sleep) well.

c) I got really sunburnt at the weekend because I _______________ (sit) in the garden too long.

d) When we got home, we realised we _______________ (forget) our key.

e) Poppy was upset because Leo _______________ (not/speak) to her all week.

f) We thought our cat _______________ (run) away, but we found it again in our neighbour's garden.

g) Julia _______________ (write) half of her essay when her computer broke down.

h) I couldn't buy the new CD I wanted because I _______________ (spend) all my pocket money.

i) The team went out to celebrate after they _______________ (win) the match.

j) Chris wrote to thank us because we _______________ (give) him a present.

k) Anna sent us copies of the photos she _______________ (take).

l) After we _______________ (buy) the ice-cream, we sat down under a tree to eat it.

Tipp Schau dir noch einmal den Klassenarbeitsauszug am Kapitelanfang an. Hier hat jemand nicht darauf geachtet, dass einige Ereignisse vor den anderen Ereignissen in der Vergangenheit lagen. Um solche Fehler zu umgehen, musst du auf den Kontext achten: Was muss als Erstes passiert sein?
Beispiele: *The dog ran away because someone had left the door open.* (Der Hund konnte nur wegrennen, weil vorher jemand die Tür aufgelassen hatte.)
It had rained so hard that the river flooded. (Der vorangehende Regen hat die Überschwemmung verursacht.)

2 Choose the correct alternatives in the following sentences.

a) My parents went/had gone to Spain in May – they won/had won the holiday in a competition.
b) After the rain had stopped/stopped, we had continued/continued our walk.
c) I decided/had decided not to see the film after Jake told/had told me the ending.
d) We were sorry when David and Cathy had moved/moved away: they had lived/lived next door to us for many years.
e) Emily had burnt/burnt the dinner, so we had ordered/ordered a pizza.
f) Everyone was/had been surprised when the team won. They didn't win/hadn't won a match for months.
g) When Columbus had discovered/discovered America, he didn't know that the Vikings had been/were there before him.
h) Zoe had/had had to stay late at school because she broke/had broken one of the rules.
i) We hadn't wanted/didn't want any dessert because we had already had/already had so much to eat.
j) Daniel didn't know/hadn't known about Lily's new boyfriend because nobody told/had told him.
k) She didn't meet/hadn't met you because you left/had left the party when she arrived/had arrived.

3 Join the two halves of the sentences below. For one part of the sentence you will need the past perfect and for the other part the simple past. Think about what happened first! There is an example to help you.

a) Our car was stolen.	We called the police.
b) Pete borrowed my book.	He lost his.
c) Jane ate a big lunch.	She wasn't hungry.
d) Gary was tired.	He ran 15 kilometres.
e) I got into trouble.	I didn't do my homework.
f) The house was very dirty.	They had a party.
g) The tree was lying on the ground.	It fell down during a storm.
h) Rob broke up with Kyra.	Kyra felt depressed.
i) Lucy was late.	She forgot to set her alarm clock.
j) Paul won a prize.	He was very happy.

Example: *a) We called the police because our car had been stolen.*

b) *Pete* ______________________ *because he* ______________________

c) ____

d) ____

e) ____

f) ____

g) ____

h) ____

i) ______________________

____

____

j) ______________________

____

____

4 "Had" or "hadn't"? Choose the best alternative for the following sentences, then add the past participle of one of the verbs below.

bake ▪ check ▪ miss ▪ post ▪ visit

a) Billy walked home because he ______ ____________ the bus.

b) I ______________________ my messages, so I didn't know what time we were meeting.

c) Max ______________________ Berlin before, so he wanted to see all the historic sites.

d) Stella was angry that Alex ______________________ the story on the Internet.

e) Josh __________________ a cake before, but it tasted really good!

Tipp Denke beim Übersetzen des *past perfect* daran, dass du das Plusquamperfekt („hatte aufgeräumt") verwendest und nicht das Perfekt („hast aufgeräumt").
Beispiel: *After Ryan had cleaned his room, he watched TV.*
FALSCH: Nachdem Ryan sein Zimmer ~~aufgeräumt hat~~, hat er ferngesehen.
RICHTIG: Nachdem Ryan sein Zimmer aufgeräumt hatte, hat er ferngesehen.

5 Translate the following sentences into German. Write the answers in your exercise book.
a) My father was born after my grandparents had moved to Canada.
b) Ben was tired after he had run 10 kilometres.
c) There was no more milk because Eva had drunk it all.
d) When the last band had played, everybody went home.

Fehler-Check

Fill the gaps in the text below. Use the past perfect or the simple past.

Seventeen-year-old Tamara Haworth was last year's winner of "A Talent for Singing". Now, one year later, she talks about her experience of winning. "I ____________ (sing) in lots of competitions before I ____________ (enter) "A Talent for Singing", but that ____________ (be) my first casting show. The hardest part of winning was becoming a celebrity overnight. Joey Cramer, who ____________ (win) the show one year before me, ____________ (give) me some good advice: "Never forget who your real friends are." This is very important! Just after the show __________ (end), a lot of girls at my school who __________________ (never/speak) to me before suddenly said they ___________ (be) my 'friend'. Some of them even _______ (tell) newspapers about things I ______________ (do); unfortunately, a lot of these stories ____________ (not/be) true. One paper even ___________ (print) a story about me and a well-known rapper – I _______________ (never/meet) the guy! At that point, I really ____________ (find) out who my true friends are, friends I ___________ (make) before I ____________ (become) famous and who I can still have a laugh with today."

☐ Fehler	0 – 3 Fehler	4 – 7 Fehler	mehr als 7 Fehler
	Super!	In Ordnung!	Bitte noch einmal üben!

Future forms I: will oder *going to?*

"What will you do this weekend?" asked Jonas. "Well, first I'll finish my II
homework, and then I'll visit my great aunt," I replied. "Wow, that I
sounds really boring!" laughed Jonas. "I'll go to see a film this evening, I
I'll buy some new clothes on Saturday morning and in the evening I
we'll have a big party at Andy's house. But I'll take you along to the I
party, too, if you will go." I

Regeln: *will future*

In dem Klassenarbeitsauszug oben wurde ausschließlich das *will future* benutzt. Im Englischen gibt es aber auch noch andere Formen, die Zukunft auszudrücken, etwa das *going to future*.
Wann benutzt man das *will future*, wann das *going to future*?

1. Das *will future* bildest du mit *will + infinitive*. Bei einer Verneinung verwendest du *won't*. Das ist die Kurzform von *will not* und wird besonders im gesprochenen Englisch häufig benutzt.
   Beispiele: *I will be ready in five minutes. Sue won't come, I guess.*

2. Das *will future* benutzt du, um über Ereignisse zu sprechen, die in der Zukunft mit (ziemlicher) Sicherheit so geschehen werden.
   Beispiel: *Ellie will turn sixteen next Monday.*

3. Das *will future* benutzt du außerdem, um anderen ein spontanes Angebot oder eine spontane Entscheidung mitzuteilen.
   Beispiel: *I'll go and make everyone a cup of coffee.*

Tipp | Oft werden Ausdrücke wie *I think*, *maybe* oder *perhaps* mit *will/ won't* benutzt. Sie signalisieren, dass der Sprecher seine Meinung ausdrückt und zukünftige Ereignisse quasi „voraussagt“.

Übungen

1 What will the world be like in the year 2210?
Complete the sentences with *will* and one of the verbs below.

be ▪ build ▪ eat ▪ grow ▪ have ▪ live ▪ run ▪ take ▪ work

a) People ______________ on the moon.

b) Cars __________________ on electricity instead of petrol.

c) Everybody ______________ their own fruit and vegetables.

d) Nobody ______________ meat.

e) Schools ______________ virtual teachers.

f) Mobile phones ____________ 10 times smaller than they are now.

g) A lot more people ________________ from home.

h) It ______________ three hours to fly to Australia from Europe.

i) We ________________ our houses of recycled material.

Tipp Das englische Verb *will* ist leicht mit dem deutschen Verb *wollen* zu verwechseln (siehe den letzten Satz des Klassenarbeitsauszugs auf S. 21). Denke also daran, dass *will* mit *werden* zu übersetzen ist! *Wollen* heißt dagegen *want to*:
Beispiele: *He will send him an e-mail this evening.*
FALSCH: Er ~~will~~ ihm heute Abend eine E-Mail schicken.
RICHTIG: Er wird ihm heute Abend eine E-Mail schicken.
I want to go out this evening.
FALSCH: Ich ~~werde~~ heute Abend weggehen.
RICHTIG: Ich will heute Abend weggehen.

2 *Werden* or *wollen*? Translate the following sentences into German!

a) I'll have a bath when I get home.

____

____

b) We'll meet Harry after school.

____

____

c) I want to go to New York one day.

____

d) I'll help you with the project.

____

e) He wants to play the guitar.

____

Regeln: *going to future*

1. Die Bausteine dieser Zukunftsform sind:
   Form von *be* im Präsens + *going to* + Verb im Infinitiv
   Beispiel: *Oh no! Phil's going to break up with Tara!*

2. *Going to* wird benutzt, wenn man Zukunftspläne oder Absichten ausdrücken will. In den ersten drei Sätzen im Klassenarbeitsauszug auf S. 21 hätte *going to* verwendet werden müssen, weil es um Pläne und nicht um spontane Entscheidungen geht.
   Beispiel: *Starting tomorrow, I'm going to do more exercise.*

3. Manchmal können wir sehen oder erahnen, was gleich/bald passieren wird, weil es bereits Anzeichen dafür gibt. Auch dann wird das *going to future* verwendet.
   Beispiel: *Nick looks really upset. I think he's going to cry.*

Tipp Benutze das ***going to future***, um über **Pläne** zu sprechen.
Bei **spontanen Entscheidungen** musst du dagegen das ***will future*** verwenden. Vergleiche die folgenden Beispiele:
"Did you know that your cousin is in town for a few days?"
"Yes, I'm going to meet her later on."
(Ich plante bereits, mich mit meiner Cousine zu treffen.)
"Did you know that your cousin is in town for a few days?"
"Really? I'll try to meet up with her while she's here."
(Ich entscheide mich spontan, meine Cousine zu treffen, als ich erfahre, dass sie in der Stadt ist.)

Übungen

3 Read Ryan's diary for next week and make sentences about his plans using going to.

Monday	5 p. m. Volleyball
Tuesday	Driving lesson after school
Wednesday	Hand in article for school magazine
Thursday	Help plan youth club summer party
Friday	Buy present for Grandma
Saturday	Grandma's 70th birthday party
Sunday	10 a. m. meet Helen – swimming pool

Example: *On Monday Ryan's going to play volleyball at 5 p. m.*

a) *On Tuesday* ____________________

b) ____________________

c) ____________________

d) ____________________

e) ____________________

f) ____________________

4 What is going to happen in the following situations? Make sentences using the verbs below.

bake ▪ begin ▪ have ▪ kiss ▪ win

Example: *Kim is carrying a tennis racket. She's going to play tennis.*

a) Alex is faster than all the other runners.

He ______________________________ the race.

b) The audience are in their seats and the orchestra is ready to play.

The concert ______________________________

c) My parents are buying lots of sausages and steaks.

They ______________________________ a barbecue.

d) Sophie's looking through her recipe books.

She ______________________________ a cake.

e) Max and Eve are standing in the corner, looking into each other's eyes. They ______________________________.

5 *Will* or *going to*? Choose the correct alternative.

a) Adam's Halloween party is in two weeks, but I already know what I will / I'm going to wear.
b) Sorry, I can't talk now. I'll / I'm going to call you back later.
c) I don't think Luis will / is going to come this evening – he doesn't really like the theatre.
d) We'll / We're going to go swimming this afternoon – would you like to come?
e) Mark will / is going to ask Amy out! I wonder what she'll / she's going to say!
f) Maybe he'll / he's going to let you borrow his laptop – why don't you ask him?
g) "Can I take your order?" "Um, OK, I'll have / I'm going to have the chicken, please."

Fehler-Check

Fill the gaps in the text below, using *will* or *going to*.

Ten years from now – what ________________________ (your life/be like)? "I think I ____________________ (enjoy) my life more in ten years than I do now", says Greg, 17. "I ________________________ (not/be) at school any more and I'm sure I ___________________________ (have) a good job. I _________________ (study) to be a computer programmer, because then I ___________________ (be) able to earn lots of money. My specialisation: I ____________________________ (design) computer games!"

Sonya, on the other hand, is not so positive about the future. "I think a lot of things ________________________ (change) in the next ten years, but not always for the better. The level of pollution in our cities _________________________ (rise) and, as a result, the quality of life ____________________ (fall). That's why I ______________________ (not/stay) in London. As soon as I have enough money, I __________________ (move) to the countryside. I ______________________ (sell) my car and go everywhere by bike. And I ____________________ (run) my own vegetarian restaurant. People _______________________ (have to) start changing the way they live if our planet ______________________ (survive)."

☐ **Fehler**	**0 – 3 Fehler** Super!	**4 – 8 Fehler** In Ordnung!	**mehr als 8 Fehler** Bitte noch einmal üben!

Future forms II: present tenses, future perfect

My best friend Rebecca will move to another town with her family I
tomorrow. Their train is leaving at 9 o'clock, and I go to the station to II
say goodbye. I hope we will stay friends – by the end of this month
we'll know each other for ten years! I'll plan to visit her in a couple of II
months. I wonder how many mails we'll send each other by the time we I
meet again!

Regeln: *present tenses with future meaning*

Auch Gegenwartsformen können verwendet werden, um über die Zukunft zu sprechen.

1. Benutze das *present progressive*, um über **feste Pläne** zu sprechen. Der Zeitpunkt oder Zeitraum für diese Vorhaben steht schon fest und wird oft mitangegeben.
   Beispiele: *My grandmother is coming to stay with us next week.*
   Where are you going on your next holiday?

   Im Klassenarbeitsauszug oben hätte zum Beispiel im ersten Satz das *present progressive (is moving)* verwendet werden müssen, da es dort um einen festen Plan geht.

2. Auch das *simple present* kann Zukunft ausdrücken. Diese Verbform benutzt man, wenn es um **unveränderliche** Zeitpunkte und Zeiträume geht, etwa bei Fahrplänen, Stundenplänen oder Öffnungszeiten.
   Beispiele: *What time does the match start?*
   Our train leaves at 8.30 a. m., so we need to leave early.

Übungen

1 Rearrange the words to make sentences using the present progressive.

a) next Melanie party a we're for weekend surprise planning

____

b) to Thursday going the I'm dentist's on

____

c) the Scotland in driving morning parents to my are

____

d) doing what you tomorrow are ?

____

e) my dinner family this with I'm boyfriend's evening having

____

2 Here is part of the Oakfield Sports Centre's summer programme. Read the statements on the next page and say whether they are true or false; if they are false, correct them!

Shape up for summer!
Mondays 5 – 6.30 p.m. from June 18th

1st – 5th August: Football for the under-10s
9 a.m. – 1 p.m., except Wednesday: 9 a.m. – 2 p.m.
Five-a-side tournament on Friday morning.

Up with the sun! Come for an early morning run with us before the day gets too hot.
Meeting point: outside the sports centre, 7 a.m., every Tuesday and Thursday in July and August.

Hope to see you there!

a) "Shape up for summer" finishes at half past six in the morning.

____

b) "Shape up for summer" begins in the middle of June.

____

c) Football for the under-10s starts on the second day of the month.

____

d) Football training finishes early on Wednesday.

____

e) The five-a-side tournament starts after lunch.

____

f) The early morning running group meets three times a week.

____

3 Simple present or present progressive?
Choose the correct verb form for the following sentences.

a) Eve ______________ (fly) to Portugal next week.

b) The course ______________ (begin) at exactly 9 a. m. – please be on time.

c) We ______________________ (study) for our French test at Lena's house after school tomorrow.

d) When ____________ the last bus ____________ (leave) for the city centre?

e) Eddie ______________ (finish) his training on 31st July.

f) Fantastic news – Alison and Matt ________________ (get married) in autumn!

g) The project ________________ (not/start) until the end of the year.

4 Which future form? Choose the correct alternative in the following sentences.

a) I'll play / I'm playing / I play football with my friends next Saturday.
b) I'm sure Philip will win / is winning / wins the match tomorrow – he's the best player.
c) The new museum will open / is opening / opens next week, and everyone in my class will go / is going / goes.
d) "Mum, can I stay up and watch the film?"
"No, it will finish / is finishing / finishes too late."
e) I'll be having / I'm having / I have my hair cut tomorrow – really short!
f) Do you know what Claire will do / is doing / does this weekend?
g) I'll drive / I'm driving / I drive home if you're too tired.
h) The concert will start / is starting / starts at eight o'clock.
i) Selina will move / is moving / moves in with her boyfriend as soon as he has found a new flat.
j) George is meeting/will meet/meets his old English teacher next Wednesday.

Regeln: *future perfect*

1. Das *future perfect* drückt Aktivitäten oder Ereignisse aus, die zu einem bestimmten Zeitpunkt in der Zukunft bereits abgeschlossen sein werden.
2. So wird das *future perfect* gebildet: *will + have + past participle*
Beispiel: *By the end of June, I will have left school.*

Übungen

5 Mike is very ambitious. Here are some of the activities he's planning to do in the future. Make sentences about what he'll have done at certain times in his life if everything goes according to plan!

At 17: form my own band
At 19: have my first hit single
At 22: start my own business
At 25: make my first million euros
At 28: write a best-selling novel
At 30: buy a penthouse in L.A.
At 33: move to a small island

Example: *By the time he's 17, he'll have formed his own band.*

a) *By the time he's 19, he* ______________________
b) ______________________
c) ______________________
d) ______________________
e) ______________________
f) ______________________

6 Make sentences using the future perfect and one of the verbs below.

eat ▪ know ▪ leave ▪ take ▪ visit

a) No, I won't be at home at 9 o'clock. I ______________________ the house by then.

b) If we don't hurry up, they ______________________ all the cake by the time we get to the party!

c) Next December my parents ______________________ each other for 25 years.

d) By the end of the summer holidays, thousands of tourists ______________________ the castle.

e) By this time next week we ______________________ our exams.

Fehler-Check

Fill the gaps in the text below, using the correct future form.

Next term I ______________________ (go) to a school in England for three weeks. My head teacher has given me permission to go because I ____________________ (not / take) any exams next term. While I'm in England, I ____________________ (stay) with a guest family.
We've been e-mailing each other for the past few weeks: they told me they ______________________ (paint) the guest room by the time I arrive, just for me! As well as this, they ____________________ (take) me on daytrips at the weekends, which is great. One attraction I really want to see is the new Roman Museum in York – it _________________ (open) in a few weeks from now.
By the time I leave, I hope I ______________________ (make) some new friends and that I __________________ (enjoy) the experience!

☐ Fehler	0 – 2 Fehler Super!	3 – 4 Fehler In Ordnung!	mehr als 4 Fehler Bitte noch einmal üben!

Zeitformen in der indirekten Rede

"I'm looking forward to the weekend," said Sally.

Sally said me she is looking forward to the weekend.

"Can you help me move this cupboard?" asked Peter.

Peter asked can you help me move this cupboard.

Regeln

Oft kommt es vor, dass wir jemandem erzählen wollen, was eine andere Person gesagt hat. Dafür benutzt man im Englischen die sogenannte *reported speech*, auch *indirect speech* genannt. Dabei muss man – anders als in dem Klassenarbeitsauszug oben – einiges im Satz ändern.

1. In den meisten Fällen geht die Verbform beim Übergang von der *direct speech* zur *reported speech* einen Schritt zurück in die Vergangenheit:

direct speech		***reported speech***
present tense (*simple* und *progressive*)	wird zu	*past tense* (*simple* und *progressive*)
past tense (*simple* und *progressive*)	wird zu	*past perfect* (*simple* und *progressive*)
present perfect (*simple* und *progressive*)	wird zu	*past perfect* (*simple* und *progressive*)

Beispiele: *"I love tennis." → He said (that) he loved tennis.*
"We're meeting at six." → Rob told me (that) they were meeting at six.

2. Achtung: *Past perfect* bleibt *past perfect*!
Beispiel: *"I'd never been to Berlin before." → She said (that) she'd never been to Berlin before.*

3. *Will* wird zu *would*, *can* zu *could*, *may* zu *might*, *must* zu *had to*.
Beispiel: *"I'll contact Joanna as soon as possible." → She told me (that) she would contact Joanna as soon as possible.*

4. In der *reported speech* kannst du das Wort *that* (deutsch: ..., *dass* ...) im Nebensatz beibehalten oder weglassen, ohne dass sich dadurch die Bedeutung des Satzes ändert – siehe die Beispiele oben.

Tipp *Say* und *tell* bedeuten „sagen, erzählen". Sie werden daher oft in der *reported speech* verwendet. Aber aufgepasst: *Tell* verlangt immer ein Objekt! Vergleiche:
She said she'd never been to Berlin before.
She told ***me*** *she'd never been to Berlin before.*

Übungen

1 Change the following sentences from direct speech to reported speech. Pay attention to the verb forms!

a) "Marcus plays the drums in a band."

She said ______________________________

b) "I learnt to ski last year."

He told ______________________________

c) "I've never eaten sushi."

He said ______________________________

d) "William's studying to be a doctor."

She told ______________________________

e) "I'll lend you my book."

Ella said ______________________________

f) "My parents are going to buy a new car."

Liam told ______________________________

g) "I can swim underwater."

She said ____

h) "You must come on time."

Our teacher told ____

i) "I may win first prize."

He said ____

Tipp Nicht vergessen: Beim Übergang in die *reported speech* müssen auch Pronomen, Zeit- und Ortsangaben verändert werden. Merke:

this → that	*my → her/his*
these → those	*our → their*
here → there	*now → then*
yesterday → the day before	*today → that day*
tomorrow → the following day	*last week → the week before*

2 Choose the correct alternative in the following sentences. Imagine you are reporting the conversations one day later.

a) "We're celebrating our exam results with a party this evening."
They said we/they/you were celebrating our/their/your exam results with a party tonight/that evening.

b) "I'll meet you back here later this afternoon."
Daniel said I'd/you'd/he'd meet you/me/him back here/there later that/this afternoon.

c) "You can't go with us, Simon."
She told me/him/you that I/we/he couldn't go with her/us/them.

d) "Please send me the information by next week at the latest."
He asked me to send me/you/him the information by next week/the following week/that week at the latest.

e) "My grandpa was upset because I forgot to send him a birthday card."
Susannah said that her grandpa had been upset because I'd/he'd/she'd forgotten to send her/them/him a birthday card.

3 "Say" or "tell"? Put in the correct verb.

a) Alan ____________ us what he'd done on his holiday.

b) My teacher ______________ my parents that I'd been late every day that week.

c) My teacher ______________ my parents had to come and see her.

d) Jessica _____________ Sean had cheated on her.

e) Jessica ______________ Sean she had cheated on him.

4 When you saw Robin last week, this is what he told you:

"I never watch TV." "I can't ride a bike."
"I'll be at home this weekend." "I love playing tennis."
"I've got two cats." "I'm going to Spain in July."

But then you find out that he told Carrie something completely different! Report what Robin told you.

Example: *Carrie: "Robin's just bought a new flat-screen TV."*
You: *"But he told me he never watched TV."*

a) Carrie: "Robin went to work by bike yesterday."

You: "But he told me ____"

b) Carrie: "Robin's going away this weekend."

You: "But ____"

c) Carrie: "Robin's not very fond of sports."

You: "____"

d) Carrie: "Robin's allergic to cats."

You: "____"

e) Carrie: "Robin never wants to go abroad."

You: "____"

Regeln: *reported questions*

Wie gibt man Fragen in indirekter Rede wieder?
- Bei *yes/no questions*: Benutze *asked/wanted to know* + *if/whether*.
- Bei *open questions*: Benutze *asked/wanted to know* + ein *question word* (z. B. *what, why*).
- *Do/did* fallen weg.

Beispiele: *"Did you see Sarah?" → He asked me whether I had seen Sarah.*
"Where do you live?" → She asked me where I lived.

Übung

5 You have found an old friend, Jacob, on a social networking website. Here are some of the questions you asked him.

Where do you live?
Have you still got your dog?
What have you been doing in the last few years?
Have you seen any of our other old friends recently?
How is your sister?
Did you ever go on your round-the-world trip?
When will you next be in town?
Can you send me your e-mail address?

Now change your questions into reported speech!

a) I asked Jacob where ______________________

b) I asked him ______________________

c) ______________________

d) ______________________

e) ______________________

f) ______________________

g) ______________________

h) ______________________

Fehler-Check

Last week, I interviewed my granny for a school project

Me: "What do you remember best about your childhood?"
Granny: "Well, I can remember playing in the streets. The world was a much safer place back then and our parents gave us much more freedom than children have now."
Me: "Do you miss the "good old days"?"
Granny: "No, I prefer living in the 21st century! For example, later on today I'm going to chat online to my brother in Australia. It won't cost me a penny and I'll be able to see him at the same time!"

I asked my grandmother ______________________________

______________________. She told me ______________________

__________________. She thought the world ____________________

__________________________ and that children's parents __________

___________________________ than ________________________.

I then asked her ____.

She replied that ____

__________________. She said that later on ____________________

____.

It ____

____.

☐ Fehler	0 – 2 Fehler **Super!**	3 – 5 Fehler **In Ordnung!**	mehr als 5 Fehler **Bitte noch einmal üben!**

Verben: Typische Hürden

Conditionals

What would it be like if you would be really poor? Imagine if you hadn't **II**
the chance to go to school, but instead would work in a factory to earn **I**
money for your family. If I wouldn't have a good education, I might not **II**
got a job and wouldn't had enough money to live off. If I was born in a **II**
country like India, this might had happened to me. **I**

Regeln: *conditional sentences type II*

Mit dem sogenannten *conditional sentence type II* beschreibt man Ereignisse oder Zustände, deren Eintreten eher unwahrscheinlich oder gar unmöglich ist.

1. Bei dieser Art von Bedingungssätzen steht der *if-clause* im ***simple past***. Im Hauptsatz steht ***would/could/might + infinitive***.
   Beispiele: *If it snowed a bit more, we could build a snowman.*
   If you ate less chocolate, you wouldn't have so many bad teeth.

2. Es kann sowohl der Hauptsatz als auch der *if-clause* an erster Stelle stehen.
   Wichtig: Wenn der *if*-Satz an erster Stelle steht, werden die beiden Sätze mit einem Komma getrennt; umgekehrt nicht.
   Beispiele: *If she had enough money, she'd buy a car.*
   She'd buy a car if she had enough money.

3. Bei dem Verb *be* musst du dir eine Besonderheit merken: Oft wird bei Bedingungssätzen *I were* statt *I was* benutzt. Beides ist korrekt.
   Beispiel: *If I was/were already 18, I would take driving lessons.*

Tipp | Der Ausdruck *If I were you* wird oft benutzt, um jemandem einen Ratschlag zu geben: *If I were you, I'd study harder for the test.*

Übungen

1 Match up the two halves of the sentences below.

a) If I lived in France,	i) we could all go to the disco.
b) If we went camping,	ii) she'd finish her work much faster.
c) If the teacher saw me sending texts in class,	iii) the world would be a better place.
d) If we visited Los Angeles,	iv) I'd be very proud of myself.
e) If Katie didn't waste so much time,	v) I'd have to speak French.
f) If my parents let me stay out late,	vi) we could go for a swim in the lake.
g) If I were you,	vii) we'd sleep in a tent.
h) If people were more friendly,	viii) she'd take my phone away.
i) If the weather was hotter,	ix) we might see some film stars.
j) If I won an Oscar,	x) I wouldn't eat so much chocolate.

Tipp

Denke daran:
Im *if-clause* darf kein *would/could/might* auftauchen (siehe die Fehler im Klassenarbeitsauszug auf S. 39).
WRONG: *If she ~~would have~~ her hair cut, she would look much better.*
RIGHT: *If she had her hair cut, she would look much better.*

2 Fill in the gaps below to make sentences using conditional type II.

a) If I ________________ (have) time, I ________________ (learn) another language.

b) We ________________ (invite) Lindsay to the party if she ________________ (be) in town.

c) If he ________________ (love) me, he ________________ (phone).

d) If you ______________ (have) a dog, you ______________ (have to) take it for walks every day.

e) If I ______________ (live) by the sea, I ______________ (swim) every morning.

f) I think you ______________ (enjoy) the film if you ______________ (see) it.

g) We ______________ (go) to the concert if the tickets ______________ (not/be) so expensive.

h) If Colin ______________ (do) more exercise, he ______________ (lose) some weight.

i) Jenny ______________ (visit) Mexico if she ______________ (speak) Spanish.

j) If my parents ______________ (find out) about the party, they ______________ (make) me stay at home for a month!

Tipp Woher weißt du, ob du einen *conditional sentence type I* oder einen *conditional sentence type II* brauchst? Du musst überlegen, ob die Bedingung, die du beschreibst, wirklich erfüllt werden kann, oder ob dies eher unwahrscheinlich oder gar unmöglich ist. Vergleiche die folgenden Beispiele:
If I have enough money, I'll buy the new "Twilight" DVD.
If I had enough money, I'd buy a sports car.
Im ersten Beispiel (*type I*) ist es realistisch zu glauben, dass die Person genug Geld für die DVD haben wird. Im zweiten Beispiel (*type II*) handelt es sich eher um einen Wunschtraum als um eine Bedingung, die wirklich erfüllbar ist.

3 Conditional sentence type I or II? Choose the most logical alternative.

a) If I am/were the Chancellor of Germany, I will/would make things better for young people.
b) A lot of the rainforest will/would disappear if we don't/didn't do more to protect it.
c) If Trisha goes/went to the party too, I won't/wouldn't speak to her.
d) If I can/could travel through time, I'll/'d visit New York in the early 19th century.
e) The city centre will/would be much cleaner if cars aren't/weren't allowed to drive there.
f) If you want/wanted to phone me later, I'll/'d be home after 4 o'clock.
g) It will/would be a real surprise if New Zealand wins/won the next World Cup!
h) If you take/took some nice photos while you're on holiday, will/would you send me some copies?
i) If you don't/didn't start writing that essay soon, it won't/wouldn't be finished on time.
j) What will/would you change about your school if you are/were head teacher for a day?
k) If you join/joined a sports club, you will/would make lots of new friends.
l) If I have/had the chance, I will/would marry Paris Hilton.

Regeln: *conditional sentences type III*

1. Der *conditional sentence type III* wird benutzt, um über Ereignisse zu sprechen, die unter bestimmten Umständen in der Vergangenheit hätten passieren (oder nicht passieren) können.

2. Der *if-clause* steht im ***past perfect***. Im Hauptsatz steht ***would/could/might + have + past participle*-Form des Verbs.**
Beispiele: *If she had run faster, she would have won the race.*
If I hadn't knocked the vase over, it wouldn't have broken.

Übungen

4 Complete the sentences with one of the verbs below.
Use conditional sentences type III.

happen ▪ like ▪ move ▪ run ▪ stay

a) If my parents had had enough money, they ____________________ to a bigger house.

b) If he hadn't got in trouble with the police, he __________ not ____________________ away.

c) If I ________________ the dress, I'd have bought it.

d) The accident ________ not __________________ if he'd been more careful.

e) If I ________________ on at school, I might have better qualifications now.

5 The following sentences describe situations that really happened.
Write down what would have happened if things had been different.
Use conditional sentences type III.
Example: *Dylan got up late, so he missed the bus.*
If Dylan hadn't got up late, he wouldn't have missed the bus.

a) We got lost because we didn't take a map with us.

____

____

b) The shop didn't have the shoes in my size, so I didn't buy them.

____

____

c) I passed my exam because my sister helped me revise.

____

____

d) Theresa was ill, so she didn't come out with us.

____

____

e) Ben had to walk home because he didn't have enough money for a taxi. ____

____

f) I didn't finish reading the book because I thought it was boring.

____

____

g) Charlotte forgot to set her alarm clock, so she didn't wake up on time. ____________________

____

____

h) Thousands of animals died because the oil tanker crashed.

____

____

Tipp Achtung: Sowohl *would* als auch *had* werden mit *'d* abgekürzt. Anhand der anderen Elemente des Satzes musst du darauf rückschließen, welches der beiden Verben gemeint sein muss.
Beispiel: *I'd have given him your message if I'd seen him. = I would have given him your message if I had seen him.*

6 *Had* or *would*? What does *'d* stand for in these sentences?

a) If we'd arrived earlier, we could have got better seats. ________

b) It might have been more interesting if they'd told us more about the history of the building. ________

c) I'd have gone out with you last night if I hadn't had such a bad headache. ________

d) If she'd contacted me sooner, I might have been able to help her. ________

e) They'd have played better if they'd trained together more often. ________________

7 In <u>some</u> of the following sentences there are mistakes in the use of the conditional. Find them and correct them.

a) What would you do if you would find a lot of money on the street?

____

b) If I had never met Rhonda, my life had been very different.

____

c) If he would have had a part-time job in the school holidays, he might have been able to come on holiday with us.

____

d) Their song would reach number 1 next week if they sold more copies. ____

Fehler-Check

Fill the gaps. Use the conditional sentences type II or type III.

This week we talk to three of our readers about moments that changed their lives, and how things ______________________ (be) different if they ________________ (make) different choices.

Emma: "If I ________________ (not/move) to London when I was 18, I ________ ________________ (not/meet) Ian and we ______________ ___________(not/get married). Also, I'm sure I ________________(not/have) my own business now if I still ________________ (live) in the village where I grew up!"

Chris: "If I ________________ (not/become) a professional tennis player, I ____________________________ (not/travel) around the world. And if I ____________________ (continue) to play, I ________________ (might/win) a Grand Slam tournament! Now I'm a tennis coach, and if I _________ (train) someone to win a big tournament, I ____________________ (celebrate) big time!"

Brian: "If my first book ____________ (be) a best-seller, I _____________ ________ (not/learn) that you have to work for success. Now I know that even if I ______ (write) a novel that nobody liked, I ______________ (can/forget) it and start again the next day. I wouldn't take it personally."

☐ Fehler	**0 – 3 Fehler** **Super!**	**4 – 8 Fehler** **In Ordnung!**	**mehr als 8 Fehler** **Bitte noch einmal üben!**

Passive voice

It worries me that clothes and other goods that sold in the west are make by children working in factories when they should be at school. Some of them have forced to work long hours just to save western companies money. Personally, I try only to buy from companies that guarantee no child labour has used.

Regeln

In manchen Fällen ist es wichtiger, eine Handlung zu betonen, als die Person, die sie durchgeführt hat. In solchen Fällen benutzt man das Passiv *(passive voice)*.

1. Das Passiv setzt sich aus folgenden Bausteinen zusammen:
   Form von *be + past participle*-Form des Verbs.
   Die folgende Tabelle zeigt dir die wichtigsten Passivkonstruktionen:

active	***passive***
Tim feeds the cats.	*The cats are fed (by Tim).*
Tim is feeding the cats.	*The cats are being fed (by Tim).*
Tim fed the cats.	*The cats were fed (by Tim).*
Tim has fed the cats.	*The cats have been fed (by Tim).*
Tim had fed the cats.	*The cats had been fed (by Tim).*
Tim will feed the cats.	*The cats will be fed (by Tim).*
Tim would/could feed the cats.	*The cats would/could be fed (by Tim).*
Tim is going to feed the cats.	*The cats are going to be fed (by Tim).*

2. Wenn du einen Satz von der Aktivform in die Passivform umschreibst, wird das Objekt des Satzes zum Subjekt.

Beispiel:

SUBJECT	VERB	OBJECT	
They	*build*	*houses.*	*(active)*
Houses	*are built.*		*(passive)*

Tipp | Wenn du einen Aktivsatz in einen Passivsatz umschreibst (oder umgekehrt), musst du manchmal das Verb vom Singular in den Plural setzen (oder umgekehrt), weil das Subjekt sich ändert.
Beispiel: *They have decorated the house. (plural verb form)*
The house has been decorated. (singular verb form)

Übungen

1 Change the following sentences from active to passive.

a) Someone cleans these rooms once a week.

____

b) Someone took this photo in Hamburg.

____

c) They're playing the match tomorrow.

____

d) The people will elect a new president next month.

____

e) Someone has stolen my bike.

____

f) They're going to finish the new road soon.

____

g) Nobody had locked the door.

____

h) They're showing the new Spielberg film next week.

____

i) Someone has broken this vase.

____

j) They repaired the computer very quickly.

____

Tipp Manchmal will man erwähnen, wer oder was die besagte Handlung durchgeführt hat. In diesem Fall benutzt man *by*.
Beispiel: *The "Harry Potter" books were written by J. K. Rowling.*
Die Betonung bleibt dabei jedoch auf dem, **was** gemacht wurde.

2 Test your knowledge! Make sentences with the correct verb form and ending.

build ▪ celebrate ▪ discover ▪ eat ▪ fight ▪ film ▪ hold ▪ invent ▪ ~~paint~~ ▪ win ▪ write

the Ancient Egyptians ▪ Captain Cook ▪ the Chinese ▪ Christians around the world ▪ Hollywood ▪ Indonesia ▪ Iraq ▪ ~~Leonardo da Vinci~~ ▪ London ▪ Shakespeare ▪ Spain

Example: *The "Mona Lisa" was painted by Leonardo da Vinci.*

a) "Macbeth" ________________ by ________________

b) Paper ________________ by ________________

c) The Gulf War ________________ against ________________

d) Australia ________________ by ________________

e) Snakes ________________ in ________________

f) The 2010 World Cup ____________________ by ____________________

g) The Pyramids ____________________ by ____________________

h) Many American TV series ____________________ in ____________________

i) Easter ____________________ by ____________________

j) The 2012 Olympic Games ____________________ in ____________________

3 Put the words in the following passive sentences in the correct order.

a) was 16th church century the in built the

____

b) cellar had the been money in hidden the

____

c) information will you the given soon be

____

d) have the been letters sent all

____

e) in damaged the had storm roof been the

____

f) Japan were cars made in these

____

g) being in premiere Berlin the held is film

____

h) will week be books next your delivered

____

Tipp *Be born* ist eine häufig benutzte Passivkonstruktion. Vergiss aber nicht: Es ist nicht möglich, jemanden zu fragen "Where are you born?", wozu die deutsche Sprache verleiten kann. Eine Frage an/über eine bestimmte Person muss immer mit der Vergangenheitsform gebildet werden, da die Geburt dieser Person ja in der Vergangenheit liegt. Vergleiche:
Where was your father born?
Most children in our town are born in the main hospital.

4 Choose the best alternative to complete the following sentences.

a) In what part of the world ______________________?

☐ is rice growing ☐ is rice grown ☐ is grown rice ☐ is growing rice

b) Mozart ______________________ in 1756.

☐ had been born ☐ is born ☐ was born ☐ were born

c) The factory ______________________ next month.

☐ will be closed down ☐ is closed down
☐ has been closed down ☐ was closed down

d) Vicky ______________________ the first prize for her painting.

☐ weren't given ☐ would be given ☐ is given ☐ should be given

e) The papers ______________________ yet.

☐ are signed ☐ haven't been signed
☐ aren't being signed ☐ won't be signed

f) The thieves got into the building because the door ______________.

☐ isn't locked ☐ was locked ☐ hadn't been locked
☐ had been locked

g) How many languages ______________________ in South Africa?

☐ is spoken ☐ are spoken ☐ are spoke ☐ are being spoken

Fehler-Check

Change these sentences from active to passive.

The police have arrested a man for stealing jewels.

A man ______________________________

Someone saw him running away from a jeweller's shop that someone had robbed a few minutes before.

He ______________________________

____

____

The thief took jewels that were worth a lot of money.

The jewels ______________________________

____

The police are now questioning the man about this and other recent jewel robberies.

____

____

They will also search his house.

____

They could send him to prison for up to 5 years.

____

☐ Fehler	**0 – 2 Fehler** Super!	**3 – 5 Fehler** In Ordnung!	**mehr als 5 Fehler** Bitte noch einmal üben!

Gerund

One way to lose weight is if you stop to eat in the evenings. I
But geting more exercise is also important. If you are interested I
to take up a sport, why not try to play a team sport: play with other III
people can help keeping you motivated. I

Regeln

1. Das *gerund* ist ein **Verb**, das ähnlich wie ein **Nomen** verwendet wird. Es besteht aus der *–ing*-Form des Verbs. In manchen Fällen bildet es das **Subjekt** des Satzes.
   Beispiele: *Skiing is a popular winter sport.*
   Walking on the grass is forbidden.

2. Das *gerund* wird auch als **Objekt** nach bestimmten Verben benutzt. Eine Gruppe solcher Verben kommt aus dem Bereich „mögen/nicht-mögen“: *like, dislike, enjoy, love, hate, can’t stand.*
   Andere Verben, die das *gerund* als Objekt bei sich haben können, sind unter anderen: *avoid, finish, imagine, mention, miss, practise, suggest.*
   Beispiele: *The dog enjoys playing with its ball.*
   You’ll have to finish doing your homework before you go out.

3. Häufig tauchen *gerund*-Formen auch bei bestimmten **Adjektiv + Präposition-Kombinationen** auf, zum Beispiel bei: *interested in, good at, keen on.*
   Beispiele: *Are you interested in learning to salsa?*
   She is really good at solving problems.

4. Zudem wird das *gerund* bei manchen **Verb + Präposition-Kombinationen** verwendet, wie: *look forward to, dream of, talk about.*
   Beispiel: *I’m looking forward to going on holiday next week.*

Übungen

1 Fill in the gaps in the following sentences using the gerund of one of the verbs below.

bake ▪ drink ▪ eat ▪ send ▪ sleep ▪ start ▪ take ▪ teach

a) ________________ coffee for breakfast helps me wake up in the morning.

b) ________________ your own cookies is a lot of fun.

c) I don't really enjoy ________________ in a tent.

d) ________________ messages is so easy nowadays – all you need is a mobile phone.

e) ________________ a walk in the fresh air will help you to concentrate better.

f) I've always loved ______________, which is why I'm planning to go to Haiti and work in a school there.

g) ________________ a new job can be quite frightening at first.

h) If you've finished ________________, put your plate in the dishwasher.

Tipp Bei bestimmten Verben musst du bei der *–ing*-Form auf die Schreibung achten. Verben, die im Infinitiv auf ein stummes *–e* enden, verlieren diesen Buchstaben in der *–ing*-Form:
have → *having*.
In anderen Fällen muss der letzte Konsonant verdoppelt werden, was etwa im obigen Klassenarbeitsauszug vergessen wurde:
get → *getting*.
Ein paar andere Ausnahmen gibt es auch (z. B. bei *lie* und *agree*): Mache die nächste Übung, um zu sehen, ob du sie kennst!

2 Write down the gerund form of the following verbs.

to lose ____________________ to shop ____________________

to clap ____________________ to lie ____________________

to win ____________________ to forget ____________________

to sit ____________________ to choose ____________________

to agree ____________________

3 Now put each of the verbs from exercise 2 into the right sentence below.

a) ____________________ the gold medal was the highlight of her sporting career.

b) When we heard the loud ________________, we knew that the concert had finished.

c) ____________________ the right place to go on holiday isn't easy.

d) Leo got into trouble for ____________________ the keys.

e) ____________________ in the sun all day is not a good idea – you'll get sunburnt!

f) I don't like ____________________ people's birthdays – that's why I always write them down.

g) She prefers ____________________ next to the window on planes.

h) I don't remember ____________________ to go with you!

i) ____________________ online isn't as much fun as going into town with your friends.

4 Match up the two halves of these sentences.

a) Wearing the right clothes is important
b) I really love relaxing
c) Please pay attention – I don't like
d) Recycling our waste
e) Being rich and famous
f) Try to avoid talking about exams
g) Sam is really good at
h) My teacher suggested having
i) The children couldn't help laughing
j) Living in the countryside

i) at the clowns.
ii) drawing pictures of people.
iii) means you need a car.
iv) for people living in extreme climates.
v) – Diane has just failed hers.
vi) repeating myself all the time.
vii) helps to protect the environment.
viii) on the beach.
ix) didn't make her happy.
x) extra maths lessons.

Regeln: *gerund* oder *to-infinitive*?

Es gibt Verben, nach denen sowohl ein *gerund* als auch ein *to-infinitive* stehen kann, z. B. *stop, remember, try*. Die Bedeutung des Satzes ändert sich jeweils. Vergleiche einmal die Bedeutungsunterschiede in den nachfolgenden Beispielen:

1. ***stop***
Beispiel: *One way to lose weight is if you stop eating in the evenings.*
So hätte der Satz in der Klassenarbeit oben lauten müssen. Er besagt, dass man abends nicht mehr essen soll. *Stop **to eat*** bedeutet dagegen, dass man mit anderen Aktivitäten aufhören soll, **um** zu essen. Das ergibt in dem Zusammenhang keinen Sinn.

2. ***remember***
Beispiele: *I remember locking the door* = Ich erinnere mich daran, wie ich die Tür abgesperrt habe (ich habe es noch vor Augen).
I remembered to lock the door = Ich habe nicht vergessen (habe daran gedacht), die Tür abzusperren.

3. ***try***
Beispiele: *If exams make you nervous, try doing some breathing exercises* = Wenn du Prüfungsangst hast, probiere es einmal mit Atemübungen.
I tried to do some breathing exercises, but I couldn't really concentrate on them = Ich habe versucht (mich bemüht), Atemübungen zu machen, aber ich konnte mich nicht wirklich darauf konzentrieren.

Übung

5 Fill the gaps with the correct form of the word in brackets: gerund or infinitive.

a) I know that Jodie's got the CD – I remember ________________ (give) it to her last week.

b) Did you remember ________________ (call) Thomas to tell him what time we're meeting?

c) Why don't you try ________________ (ask) at your local library?

d) He tried several times ________________ (contact) Erica but she never answered her phone.

e) We stopped ________________ (talk) to a friend on the way to the station and nearly missed our train.

f) Please stop ________________ (talk) – I can't hear what she's saying.

Fehler-Check

Read Dave's blog and fill the gaps with the gerund or infinitive.

Saturday. Very tired, so ______________ (get) up wasn't easy, but I don't like ____________ (be) late on days like this. And it was a big day: our demonstration in the city centre! _______________ (show) the government that they must do more to protect the environment is really important, I believe. I even remembered ______________ (take) my huge "Green World" flag along. The organisers were interested in _____________ (see) if any local politicians would turn up. Several members of the Green Party were there, of course, but some of the others seemed to be afraid of ______________ (meet) the demonstrators and _____________ (listen) to their concerns – typical! __________ (march) through the city was great, as we got lots of media attention. We even stopped ____________ (hand in) a petition at the parliament building. A long day – looking forward to _________ (have) a nice long sleep tomorrow morning.

Sunday. I normally love _____________ (lie) for hours in bed, but today ...

☐ **Fehler**	**0 – 2 Fehler** **Super!**	**3 – 5 Fehler** **In Ordnung!**	**mehr als 5 Fehler** **Bitte noch einmal üben!**

Phrasal verbs

Look to the sunset! Isn't it beautiful?

I'm looking at my phone – have you seen it?

If you don't know what the word means, look at it in a dictionary.

We don't need the light on – you can switch off it now.

Regeln:

1. *Phrasal verbs* sind Verbindungen aus **Verb + Präposition** oder aus **Verb + Adverb**. Die Bedeutung des Verbs ändert sich, je nachdem mit welcher Präposition oder welchem Adverb es kombiniert wird.
   Beispiele: *Look at the sunset!* (*look at* = anschauen)
   I'm looking for my phone. (*look for* = suchen)
   If you don't know what the word means, look it up in a dictionary. (*look s.th. up* = etwas nachschlagen)

2. Wenn das *phrasal verb* ein Objekt hat, kann dieses in der Regel sowohl **vor** als auch **nach** der Präposition bzw. dem Adverb stehen.
   Beispiele: *Turn off the television. Turn the television off.*
   Why don't you take off your coat and sit down?
   Why don't you take your coat off and sit down?

3. Achtung: Wenn das Objekt ein Pronomen ist (z.B. *her, it, them* etc.), muss es **vor** der Präposition bzw. dem Adverb stehen.
   Beispiele:
   WRONG: Please turn ~~off it~~.
   RIGHT: Please turn it off.

Übungen

1 Complete these sentences with one of the phrasal verbs below. Make sure you use the correct tense.

ask for ▪ break down ▪ come in ▪ fall off ▪ get up ▪ go out ▪ grow up ▪ pay for ▪ set out ▪ slow down ▪ try on ▪ wait for

a) Richard ________________ so late this morning that he didn't even come to school.

b) Nice to see you again! Please ________________!

c) Can you ________________ my coffee? I've left my purse at home.

d) Maddie doesn't want to ________________ with us this evening.

e) I'm tired of ________________ Alison. Let's just go without her.

f) Please ________________! The speed limit here is only 30 kilometres an hour.

g) ________________ these trousers. I'll buy them for you if they fit.

h) She ________________ in a small village in the heart of the English countryside.

i) Our car ________________ on the motorway last weekend.

j) I was so happy when Eric ________________ my phone number!

k) "How did you break your arm?"
"I ________________ a wall."

l) They ________________ just after breakfast and arrived at lunchtime.

2 Choose the best alternative in the following sentences.

a) Take on/off/out your jacket and have a seat.
b) I need to take my books back/in/out to the library.
c) Darren is going off/out/over with Michelle.
d) Is Ava here? I need to talk to/at/over her.
e) Please fill off/on/in this form and return it by Friday.
f) When is Mary coming in/over/back from her holiday?
g) If you write it up/down/on, it'll help you remember it.
h) Would you like to come in/round/through this evening? We could get a pizza.
i) I've been feeling a lot more relaxed since I took on/over/up yoga.
j) Watch out/by/off! You nearly stepped on my foot!

3 Match up the sentences with a similar meaning.

a) Put on your clothes.
b) They've put off their wedding for 6 months.
c) We've run out of milk.
d) Let's eat out tonight.
e) My father's trying to give up smoking.
f) Could you speak up, please? I can't hear you.
g) Hmm, I don't think that shirt really goes with those trousers, to be honest.
h) The conference is taking place in the Royal Radcliffe Hotel.
i) We were all surprised when my cousin turned up at our house.
j) I don't believe Lucas' story – I think he made it up.

i) The event is happening there.
ii) He's trying to stop.
iii) Get dressed.
iv) They don't look good together.
v) He didn't tell the truth.
vi) There isn't any left.
vii) She arrived suddenly.
viii) They're doing it later than planned.
ix) Say it louder.
x) Why don't we go to a restaurant?

Tipp Die Bedeutung eines *phrasal verbs* kann man sich nicht dadurch erschließen, dass man seine einzelnen Bestandteile übersetzt. Man muss *phrasal verbs* nachschlagen und auswendig lernen. Du kannst dir zum Beispiel mögliche Kombinationen mit einem bestimmten Verb merken, etwa *get up, get off, get on, get out, get in*. Oder du lernst die Kombinationen mit einer bestimmten Präposition oder einem bestimmten Adverb auswendig: *get up, look up, pick up, wake up*.

4 Correct any mistakes you find in the word order of the following sentences (not all of them contain mistakes).

a) My brother woke up me playing loud music first thing this morning.

____

b) I've finished with this now – you can take away it.

____

c) Your shoes are really dirty. Please take them off before you come into the house.

____

d) This heater's very hot – can you turn down it, please?

____

e) Ray arrives at 6 o'clock this evening, so I'll be able to pick up him after work.

____

f) Ginny didn't do her homework, so the teacher told off her.

____

g) The tree is too big now – we'll have to cut down it.

____

Tipp In manchen Fällen kann ein *phrasal verb* auch mehr als eine Bedeutung haben. Es empfiehlt sich daher, *phrasal verbs* zusammen mit Beispielsätzen zu lernen, damit die Bedeutung klar ist:
Beispiele: *Get on the 221 bus to North Finchley.*
Annie and her sister just don't get on – they're always fighting.

5 Which verb is missing from these pairs of sentences? Make sure you use the correct tense.

take ▪ get ▪ give ▪ go ▪ put ▪ come ▪ look

a) ____________ over at 8 o'clock – we'll be home by then.

Angie ____________ up with a really good idea for our project.

b) Our school is ____________ on a production of "Romeo and Juliet" next week.

This box is really heavy – I have to ____________ it down.

c) She ____________ up, had a shower and cleaned her teeth.

It took her a long time to ____________ over her grandfather's death.

d) What's that noise? It sounds like the fire alarm is ____________ off.

We're ____________ away for a few days – to Paris!

e) Please ____________ out the rubbish if you're going downstairs.

More than 300 people ____________ part in the event.

f) You can do it! Don't ____________ up now!

He finally ____________ in and bought the children the computer game they'd been asking for.

g) I'm ____________ for a birthday present for my dad.

We ____________ at the map but we couldn't find their house.

Fehler-Check

Fill in the gaps with one of the words below.

Flying abroad

back ▪ check ▪ down ▪ get ▪ go ▪ off ▪ pick ▪ put ▪ sit ▪ takes ▪ through (2x) ▪ to

a) ____________ in your bags at the check-in desk.

b) Go ____________ passport control and the security check.

c) Your hand luggage is ______________ through the x-ray machine.

d) You get your hand luggage ______________ on the other side of the machine.

e) Sit ____________ in the departure lounge until your flight is called.

f) ________________ on the plane and find your seat.

g) ____________ down and fasten your seatbelt.

h) Listen _______________ the safety instructions.

i) The plane _______________ off.

j) The plane lands. Get _______________ the plane.

k) Go __________________ passport control again.

l) ________________ up your suitcases at baggage claim.

m) ______________ out of the airport and enjoy your holiday!

☐ Fehler	0 – 2 Fehler Super!	3 – 5 Fehler In Ordnung!	mehr als 5 Fehler Bitte noch einmal üben!

Used to oder *be used to*?

I was used to going to school in a small village, but last year we moved to a big city. I had to get used to do lots of things differently at my new school. For example, I was used to be in a class with only 15 other pupils, but now there are 5 classes of 35 pupils each! At my old school, I used to knowing everybody, but not any more ...

Regeln: *used to*

1. Du benutzt *used to + infinitive*, um über frühere Gewohnheiten oder Zustände zu sprechen, die inzwischen beendet sind.
   Beispiele: *I used to play a lot of football, but now I prefer tennis.*
   They used to be very rich, but then they lost all their money.
2. Fragen und Verneinungen werden so wie bei allen anderen *simple past*-Formen gebildet.
   Beispiele: WRONG: *Where did you ~~used~~ to live?*
   RIGHT: *Where did you use to live?*
   WRONG: *She didn't ~~used~~ to have long hair.*
   RIGHT: *She didn't use to have long hair.*

Übungen

1 Put in the correct form of *used to* (question, positive or negative statement) and one of the verbs below.

go ▪ like ▪ live ▪ run ▪ smoke ▪ write

a) My father ____________________, but he gave up about 10 years ago.

b) Charlie ____________________ more than 20 kilometres a week until he injured his knee.

c) "Where ____________ you __________________ to school?" "Knoxfield High School."

d) I _________________________ olives, but now I eat them all the time!

e) People _______________________ a lot of letters before e-mail was invented.

f) "_____________ you ________________ in Berlin?" "No, in Dresden."

Regeln: *be/get used to*

Ein häufiger Fehler ist es, *used to* mit *be used to* oder *get used to* zu verwechseln. *Be used to* bedeutet, dass man an etwas gewöhnt ist. *Get used to* bedeutet, dass man dabei ist, sich an etwas zu gewöhnen. Vergleiche die folgenden Beispiele:

I used to get up early, but now I often sleep late. (Früher stand ich immer früh auf, jetzt schlafe ich oft aus.)

I'm used to getting up early. (Ich bin daran gewöhnt, früh aufzustehen.)

I'm getting used to getting up early. (Ich gewöhne mich daran, früh aufzustehen.)

Tipp Denke daran, dass du für *be/get used to* die *–ing*-Form des Verbs brauchst!

Beispiele: *I'm not used to living in the countryside.*
He isn't used to washing his own clothes.

2 Choose the correct alternative in the following sentences.

a) It was difficult in the big city at first, but now I ….
□ used to live there □ am used to living there □ am used to live there

b) I … the piano, but I don't really have time nowadays.
□ used to play □ got used to playing □ am used to playing

c) "I hope you don't mind our dog." "No, it's OK – I … animals.
□ used to □ am used to □ get used to

d) Susie … my best friend when we were at school.
□ used to be □ was used to being □ got used to being

e) The new computer program was easy to follow, so we … with it very quickly.
□ were used to working □ got used to working □ use to work

f) It isn't easy to … in a completely different culture.
□ get used to living □ be used to living □ used to live

g) Jimmy has really changed: he … so arrogant.
□ wasn't used to being □ didn't use to be □ didn't get used to being

h) I … reading until I discovered the "Harry Potter" series.
□ didn't use to enjoy □ didn't get used to enjoy □ wasn't used to enjoying

i) When you start your new school you'll have to … lots of homework every evening.
□ used to do □ get used to doing □ be used to doing

3 Correct the mistakes in the following sentences. Write the answers in your exercise book.

a) Did you used to be a Justin Bieber fan, too?

b) Elena is used to speak Italian – she goes to Italy every summer.

c) Anyone who lives in Britain is use to rain!

d) I didn't used to eat vegetables when I was a child.

e) He was used to be a famous movie star, but now nobody remembers his name.

f) Her family returned from South Africa because they couldn't be used to the climate.

Fehler-Check

Fill the gaps with *used to*, *be used to* or *get used to*.

The secret of my success: athletics champion Angie Collins

"Even when I was very young, I ____________________ (love) running and jumping, and I found out that I had a natural talent for athletics. From the age of 8, I ______________________ (train) every weekend, although I ______________________ (not/think) of it like that: as far as I was concerned, I was just having fun. Nobody was more surprised than me when I won my first junior title, but then I started to ____________________ (be) a winner and I realised I loved that feeling. At first, that was what _________ _______________ (motivate) me, but not any more. Now that I take part in several competitions a year, I _______________________ (win) just some of the time. Nowadays, I try to be a role model, too. I go and talk to young people about how important it is to ____________________ (take) regular exercise from a young age. It's great when someone tells me they _______ _______________ (not/do) any sport at all until I inspired them to start exercising!"

☐ **Fehler**	**0 – 2 Fehler** Super!	**3 – 4 Fehler** In Ordnung!	**mehr als 4 Fehler** Bitte noch einmal üben!

Häufige Fehler rund ums Nomen

3

Countable und *uncountable nouns*

The furnitures in their house are really old and dark, but my ||
grandparents don't want to spend a money on new ones. ||
As well as this, they are always complaining that there is a |
loud traffic outside their house, but they don't want to move.
But I guess much old people don't like change. |

Regeln

1. Was genau ist mit *countable* und *uncountable nouns* gemeint? Ein ***countable noun*** bezeichnet etwas, was zählbar ist. Es kann sowohl im Singular als auch im Plural benutzt werden: *an apple; three apples*.
Ein ***uncountable noun*** bezeichnet dagegen etwas, was nicht gezählt werden kann. Es darf in der Regel nur im Singular verwendet werden.
Beispiele: RIGHT: *There is a lot of snow on the ground.*
WRONG: *There are three ~~snows~~ on the ground.*

2. ***Countable nouns*** können einen unbestimmten Artikel (*a/an*) haben; ***uncountable nouns*** meistens nicht. Allerdings werden ***uncountable nouns*** oft mit *a ... of* verwendet:
Beispiele: *I love chocolate.* (kein Artikel)
Would you like a piece of this chocolate? (a ... of)

3. Achtung: Manche Nomen können sowohl als *uncountable nouns* als auch als *countable nouns* verwendet werden, je nachdem, ob etwas **Allgemeines** oder etwas **Konkretes** gemeint ist.
Beispiele: *Cola is one of the most popular drinks in the world.* (gemeint ist Cola im Allgemeinen)
I'm going to get a cola. (gemeint ist eine konkrete Cola)

Übungen

1 What goes together? Match up the two parts of these combinations:

a) a piece of	i) ice hockey
b) a cup of	ii) lightning
c) a glass of	iii) air
d) a sheet of	iv) advice
e) a spoonful of	v) rain
f) a breath of fresh	vi) wine
g) a slice of	vii) sugar
h) a game of	viii) tea
i) a shower of	ix) bread
j) a flash of	x) paper

2 Fill in the gaps with one of the words below. Add an indefinite article (a/an) only if necessary.

accident ▪ cheese ▪ film ▪ jacket ▪ meat ▪ music ▪ sandwich ▪ television ▪ weather ▪ work

a) David doesn't like ________________. He never watches it.

b) What ____ terrible ______________! It hasn't stopped raining all day.

c) I'm hungry. I'm going to make myself __________________.

d) We could hear ____ lovely __________ coming from an open window.

e) No, I don't eat ________________. I'm a vegetarian.

f) It's really cold today. Put on __________________ before you go out.

g) It took Annie a long time to find _____________ after she left school.

h) We saw ____ interesting ____________ about space travel last week.

i) Jane has had ______________________!

She's broken her arm.

j) __________________ can be made from

cows' milk or goats' milk.

Tipp Es gibt einige Nomen, die im Englischen *uncountable* sind, im Deutschen aber nicht. Dazu zählen unter anderem *information*, *hair*, *advice*, *weather*, *luck*. Diese Nomen werden im Gegensatz zum Deutschen in der Regel ohne unbestimmten Artikel und im Singular verwendet. Achtung: Das Wort *news* hat zwar ein *–s* am Ende, wird aber wie ein Singularwort gebraucht.
Beispiele: *She brushed her hair.* (nicht: *hairs*)
"That's great news!" (nicht: *Those are*)

3 Which of the following sentences need an indefinite article (*a*/*an*)?

a) Do you drink ____ coffee? I don't

b) Would you like ____ coffee? Fiona's just gone to make one.

c) "We're going on holiday tomorrow." "Have ____ good time!

d) Sorry, I won't have ____ time to help you. I've got too much homework.

e) Walking on the Great Wall of China was ____ amazing experience.

f) You really need ____ experience to do this job well.

g) Here's ____ glass. The drinks are in the kitchen – help yourself!

h) The church windows are made of ____ special coloured glass.

i) My sister's got ____ long blond hair.

j) The Internet helps people to get ____ important information.

k) The chairs are made of ____ wood.

Regeln: Mengenangaben

A lot of kann sowohl bei *countable* als auch bei *uncountable nouns* verwendet werden. Andere Mengenangaben jedoch nicht:

Mengenangabe	*uncountable noun*	*countable noun*
a lot of (viele, viel)	möglich: *a lot of help*	möglich: *a lot of keys*
much (viel)	möglich: *much love*	nicht möglich
many (viele)	nicht möglich	möglich: *many trees*
(a) little (wenig)	möglich: *little interest*	nicht möglich
(a) few (wenige)	nicht möglich	möglich: *a few horses*

Übungen

4 Choose the best way to complete these sentences.

a) Hurry up! We don't have ... time.
☐ many ☐ much ☐ few

b) The news ... good. Thousands of animals have died in the forest fire.
☐ aren't ☐ is ☐ isn't

c) I need ... about working abroad.
☐ some information ☐ some informations ☐ an information

d) You'll have to ask for ... before you use this equipment.
☐ a permission ☐ any permission ☐ permission

e) There are too ... new words to learn – I'll never remember all of them.
☐ much ☐ many ☐ a lot of

f) By the end of the holiday, they only had ... money left.
☐ a few ☐ a little ☐ much

g) I lost my purse while I was out shopping, but I found it again before it got stolen. That was ...!
☐ a real piece of luck ☐ a real luck ☐ real luck

h) Does this machine use ... electricity?
☐ many ☐ a few ☐ much

i) Can I give you ... advice? It's not a good idea to hang out with Gary and his friends.
☐ an ☐ much ☐ some

j) If we hung ... pictures on the wall, this room would look much nicer.
☐ a few ☐ a little ☐ any

k) When there is ... rain, our local river sometimes floods.
☐ many ☐ a lot of ☐ a little

5 Find the countable and uncountable nouns that go together. You will need an indefinite article or a plural form for the countable nouns.

car ▪ furniture ▪ job ▪ lamp ▪ light ▪ ~~luggage~~ ▪ music ▪ song ▪ ~~suitcases~~ ▪ sunny day ▪ table ▪ traffic ▪ weather ▪ work

Beispiel: *Did you take much luggage on holiday with you?*
No, we only took two suitcases.

a) "Is your brother still looking for __________ for the school holidays?"
"No, he's got ____________ now in our local supermarket."

b) My parents like old __________________. They have ____________ from the 18th century.

c) There used to be heavy _______________ in our town, but now ____________ have been banned from the centre.

d) Have you got enough ____________ to read your book? Why don't you switch on ________________?

e) I've always loved ___________. I've even started writing ___________ myself, but I only sing them when I'm alone!

f) We had beautiful ____________________ for our picnic – it was ______________________.

Fehler-Check

Choose the correct alternative in the following sentences.

Suzie writes: I really need an advice/a piece of advice. Everybody says I'm really good at a music/music and I'd love to take part in a casting show/casting show. Problem/The problem is my parents, who say I'm too young (I'm 15). I sent off for all the informations/information, and I discovered I need permission/a permission from my parents to audition. They don't listen when I tell them this is dream/a dream of mine. Please help!

Kay answers: Sorry, but the bad news is/are: I agree with your parents. A career in the music business is a hard work/hard work. Even if you are very musical, you also need a luck/luck to become really successful, and you must be tough, which isn't easy for a teenager/teenager. You say you have talent/a talent; well, that won't disappear in the next few years. Work on your music, but get education/an education, too. Then you'll still be able to get a job/job if, like most people, you don't instantly have a number one hit!

☐ **Fehler**	**0 – 2 Fehler** **Super!**	**3 – 5 Fehler** **In Ordnung!**	**mehr als 5 Fehler** **Bitte noch einmal üben!**

Pair nouns und andere Ausnahmen

I spend most of my pocket money on clothes: a new trouser, I
a jacket, one or two jeans. The last jeans I bought was really II
expensive: it took me a long time to save up for it! But I think it's I
important to look good and follow the latest fashions. Once I
bought a sunglasses that I saw in a magazine, and I wore them I
all the time, even though it was winter!

Regeln: *pair nouns*

1. *Pair nouns* (Paarwörter) bezeichnen Gegenstände, die aus zwei Teilen bestehen. Zu diesen Nomen gehören zum Beispiel: *pyjamas, shorts, tights, trousers, binoculars, jeans, scissors. Pair nouns* kommen nur im Plural vor.
   Beispiele: *I love her new sunglasses – they are really cool!*
   I can't find my binoculars. Have you seen them?

2. Um eine Singular-Form zu bilden, benutzt man (*a*) *pair of* + Nomen.
   Beispiele: *She always keeps a pair of sunglasses in the car.*
   I don't know which pair of jeans I should wear.

3. Wenn du *pair nouns* mit Zahlwörtern *(one, two, three ...)* verwenden möchtest, musst du ebenfalls *pair of* bzw. den Plural *pairs of* verwenden. Du darfst hier nicht wörtlich aus dem Deutschen übersetzen, wie es oben in dem Klassenarbeitsauszug getan wurde!
   Beispiele: WRONG: *I bought ~~two new trousers~~ last week.*
   RIGHT: *I bought two new pairs of trousers last week.*

Übung

1 Complete the sentences with one of the nouns below. You will need to use them more than once. Add *a pair of* if necessary.

glasses ▪ scissors ▪ shorts ▪ tights ▪ trousers

a) We all dressed up as ballet dancers for Carnival – we even wore bright pink ______________________________!

b) A shirt, a skirt, a ____________________ and smart, high-heeled boots: the perfect autumn outfit.

c) I think I need a new __________________________________ – I can hardly see a thing!

d) She got her first ________________________ when she was only 7 years old and, like most children, didn't really enjoy wearing them.

e) These ______________________ are perfect for a hot summer day.

f) I need a______________________________ to cut out this picture.

g) Be careful with those __________________________________ – they're very sharp.

h) Oh no! My _______________________________ have got a hole in the knee!

Regeln: Nomen mit unregelmäßigen Pluralbildungen

1. Manche Nomen ändern ihre Form im Plural nicht. Dazu gehören einige Nomen, die auf –*s* enden, zum Beispiel *series, means, species*, sowie einige Tiernamen, wie zum Beispiel *sheep und fish*.
Beispiele: *"Dr. Who" is a popular British drama series.*
Only three series of the sitcom were made, but it is still shown on television today.

2. Die Nomen *police* (Polizei) und *people* (Menschen, Leute) besitzen keine Plural-Endung, werden aber immer mit einer Plural-Verbform verwendet.
Beispiele: *The police have arrested the bank robbers.*
Look at the people over there – they look really strange.

Übungen

2 Correct the mistakes in the following sentences.

a) My granny wasn't very happy when I wore an old dirty jeans to her birthday party. ____________________

b) Don't panic – the police is on its way! ____________________

c) That trousers doesn't go with that orange shirt. ____________________

d) Pass me the scissor, please. ____________________

e) There are too many peoples in this room. I'm going outside for some fresh air. ____________________

f) Nobody recognised him at first as he was wearing a glasses.

____

g) I once had a pair of pyjama with a big pink rabbit on the front!

____

3 Choose the correct alternative from the underlined verbs.

a) The police is/are still looking for the jewel thieves.
b) This is/are a very rare species of bird.
c) That was/were a very expensive pair of jeans in that shop.
d) Scissors is/are dangerous for small children, so they should always be kept in a safe place.
e) There is/are many means of transport in China, but bikes are one of the most popular.
f) The new series is/are on late at night because it's very violent.

Fehler-Check

Choose the correct alternative to complete the sentences.

Summer camp rules:

* You should bring 2 waterproof trousers/pairs of waterproof trousers
* Bring some shorts/a short, but also long trousers/a long trouser in case the weather turns cool
* Jeans is/Jeans are good for wearing on hikes, as they are thick and will protect your legs from cuts and scratches.
* The nights can be cold, so pack some warm pyjamas/a warm pyjama to wear inside your sleeping bag
* Don't forget sunscreen and a sunglasses/sunglasses
* You may bring a nail scissor/a pair of nail scissors; knives are not permitted
* No more than 10 people/peoples are allowed to be in a tent at any one time
* The best means/mean of communication with your family is a cell phone, although you will only be allowed to use it at certain times
* Do bring a binocular/a pair of binoculars for observing birds and other wildlife
* We hope you enjoy your stay!

☐ Fehler	0 – 2 Fehler Super!	3 – 5 Fehler In Ordnung!	mehr als 5 Fehler Bitte noch einmal üben!

Reflexivpronomen: Die häufigsten Fehler

The other day, my brother hurt him while he was walking along the street with a friend. He was talking on his phone, so he wasn't concentrating himself and walked right into a tree! He was OK, though; in fact, when it happened, he and his friend just looked at themselves and laughed!

Regeln: *reflexive pronouns*

1. Ein *reflexive pronoun* (Reflexivpronomen) ist ein Pronomen, das auf *–self* (Singular) oder *–selves* (Plural) endet, wie zum Beispiel *himself* oder *themselves*. Es wird benutzt, wenn das Subjekt und das Objekt einer Handlung dieselbe Person sind.
   Beispiele: *Jane was talking to herself.* (*Jane* ist Subjekt und Objekt)
   They made themselves comfortable. (*They* ist Subjekt und Objekt)

2. Pronomen mit der Endung *–self/–selves* kommen im Englischen auch dann vor, wenn im Deutschen kein *selbst* steht. Ein typischer Fehler ist es, in solchen Fällen statt des *reflexive pronoun* ein nicht-reflexives Pronomen wie *me, him, her* zu verwenden.
   Beispiel: *Ich habe mich beim Snowboarden verletzt.*
   WRONG: *I injured ~~me~~ while I was snowboarding.*
   RIGHT: *I injured myself while I was snowboarding.*

3. Achtung: Nicht alle Verben, die im Deutschen ein Reflexivpronomen brauchen, benötigen auch im Englischen eines.
   Beispiel: Ich kann mich nicht konzentrieren.
   WRONG: *I can't concentrate ~~myself~~.*
   RIGHT: *I can't concentrate.*

Übungen

1 Write out the reflexive pronouns that go with the following:

a) I ____________________ b) you ____________________

c) he ____________________ d) she ____________________

e) it ____________________ f) we ____________________

g) you (plural) ____________ h) they ____________________

2 Now complete the following sentences with one of the pronouns above. You will need some of the pronouns more than once.

a) If you're thirsty, get ___________ a glass of water.

b) Emma burnt ___________ when she picked up the hot dish.

c) The children went upstairs, washed ___________ and cleaned their teeth.

d) I wrote ___________ a note so that I wouldn't forget to phone Dan.

e) We took a photo of ___________ at Buckingham Palace using the self-timer on our camera.

f) You should all be very proud of ___________ you've done a great job!

g) The town has made ___________ famous by selling its locally made ice-cream throughout the country.

h) I painted a picture of ___________ – it's a self-portrait.

i) Patrick made a video of ___________ singing and playing the guitar, and uploaded it onto the Internet.

Tipp Merke dir folgende typische Fehlerquellen beim Übersetzen vom Deutschen ins Englische:

	WRONG	RIGHT
sich die Hände waschen	~~wash yourself the hands~~	wash your hands
sich duschen	~~shower yourself~~	have a shower
sich kämmen	~~comb yourself~~	comb your hair
sich (gut) fühlen	~~feel yourself (good)~~	feel (good)

3 What goes together? Match up the sentences below.

a) Oh no! I've locked myself out!
b) They renovated the old farmhouse by themselves.
c) Help yourselves to food and drink.
d) "Where did you learn to play the guitar?"
e) If there's a technical problem,
f) "I love Judy's new dress."
g) Our drama teacher filmed us performing the play,
h) "I'm going to Prague for the weekend."
i) Come in and sit down!
j) The children went for a swim in the lake,

i) "I taught myself."
ii) Make yourselves at home!
iii) and afterwards we watched ourselves on DVD.
iv) How am I going to get back into the house?
v) then dried themselves on a towel.
vi) You'll find plates, knives and forks over there.
vii) "I hope you enjoy yourself!"
viii) Nobody helped them.
ix) the computer will switch itself off automatically.
x) "Yes, and do you know what? She made it herself!"

Tipp Nicht vergessen: *Ich kann das alleine (tun)* wird entweder mit *I can do it by myself* oder mit *I can do it on my own* übersetzt.
Beispiel: *"Do you need help?" "No, I can do it by myself."*

Regel: *each other*

Each other drückt im Gegensatz zum Reflexivpronomen eine **wechselseitige** Beziehung aus. Es wird verwendet, wenn zum Beispiel zwei oder mehr Personen etwas miteinander machen.
Beispiele: *They looked at each other.* (Sie sahen sich (gegenseitig) an.)
They looked at themselves in the mirror. (Sie sahen sich im Spiegel an.)

Übungen

4 Each other or reflexive pronoun? Choose the correct alternative.

a) Terri likes Jo, and Jo likes Terri. They like themselves/each other.
b) Mia and Ryan have split up, and now they're not even talking to themselves/each other.
c) In my family we all give ourselves/each other presents at Christmas.
d) We went into the kitchen to make ourselves/each other something to eat.

e) They met again after nearly 40 years, but in all that time they never forgot themselves/each other.
f) My mother phones her brother in Canada once a month and they tell themselves/each other all their news.
g) We hated ourselves/each other when we first met, but now we're best friends.
h) My sister and I have no secrets – we tell ourselves/each other everything.
i) Romeo and Juliet killed themselves/each other because they loved themselves/each other so much.
j) The food was placed on the table in large bowls and everybody helped themselves/each other.

Tipp Folgende Sätze werden häufig gebraucht – und oft falsch übersetzt.

	WRONG	RIGHT
Wir treffen uns um 19 Uhr.	~~We meet us at 7 p.m.~~	We're meeting at 7 p.m.
Wir sehen uns nächste Woche.	~~We'll see us next week.~~	I'll see you next week./ See you next week.

5 What is the best way to complete the following sentences?

a) Where shall we ...? At the bus stop?
☐ meet us ☐ meet each other ☐ meet

b) I like to ... every morning.
☐ have a shower ☐ shower me ☐ shower myself

c) Sean isn't coming with us because he doesn't ....
☐ feel himself well ☐ feel well ☐ feel him well

d) I haven't seen my cousin for years, but we always ... a birthday card.
☐ send ourselves ☐ send each other ☐ send us

e) She decorated the whole living room ....
☐ by herself ☐ by her own ☐ only her

f) Have a great holiday – ... when you get back!
☐ we'll see us ☐ we'll see ourselves ☐ I'll see you

g) I could ... better if you stopped playing that loud music.
☐ concentrate me ☐ concentrate ☐ concentrate myself

h) I'm just going to ... and then I'll be ready to go.
☐ comb my hair ☐ comb myself ☐ comb me the hair

i) The children need to ... before we eat.
☐ wash them the hands ☐ wash themselves the hands
☐ wash their hands

j) She is old enough to dress ... now.
☐ her ☐ herself ☐ by her own

Fehler-Check

Fill in the gaps with a reflexive pronoun *(myself, yourself, himself etc.)* or *each other*.

My great-grandmother grew up as one of 12 children. She had to do a lot of things by ______________ , such as dress ______________, from a young age. Her father was a baker, who worked for ______________ in his own shop. Her mother worked too, so the older children had to stay at home and play with ______________ until she finished work. "Because my parents didn't have much time, I became very independent. I taught ______________ to cook and sew, and made a lot of my clothes ______________. One day my friend Jenny said: 'Why don't you buy ______________ a sewing machine? Then you could make enough clothes to sell. We could even start our own company!' I would never have thought of that ______________, but Jenny and I had known ______________ for many years then, and we trusted ______________. So that's how our clothing company got started – unusual for the time, as women didn't often run businesses ______________ back then. We never became millionaires, but we were quite successful and very proud of ______________ for what we'd achieved!"

☐ **Fehler**	**0 – 2 Fehler** Super!	**3 – 5 Fehler** In Ordnung!	**mehr als 5 Fehler** Bitte noch einmal üben!

Fehlerquelle Adjektiv und Adverb

Die Satzstellung von Adjektiven

Hi, I'm Tom and I'm new to the area. I'm a 14-year-old thin tall I
boy with dark short hair and blue big eyes. I'm into science- III
fiction American films and read a lot of books by different
fantasy British writers. I spend quite a lot of time on the Internet, I
but I prefer to meet up with friends in person. So if you're a
teenage local sci-fi fan like me who's looking for new friends, I
I'd love to hear from you!

Regeln

1. Manchmal möchte man mehr als ein Adjektiv benutzen, um ein Nomen zu beschreiben. In solchen Fällen gibt es für die Adjektive eine bestimmte Reihenfolge. Wird diese Reihenfolge nicht eingehalten, klingt der Satz sehr unnatürlich, wie der Klassenarbeitsauszug oben deutlich zeigt: Obwohl die Sätze noch klar verständlich sind, klingen sie nicht gerade sehr „englisch".
   Beispiele: WRONG: *a ~~blue small~~ car*
   RIGHT: *a small blue car*

2. Adjektive können in zwei Hauptgruppen aufgeteilt werden: *opinion adjectives*, die eine Meinung über etwas oder jemanden ausdrücken (z. B. *beautiful*), und *fact adjectives*, die beispielsweise die Größe oder das Alter beschreiben (z. B. *large*). Ein *opinion adjective* kommt vor einem *fact adjective*.
   Beispiele: *a lazy old dog*
   a lovely sunny day

3. Die natürlichste Reihenfolge für *fact adjectives* ist wie folgt:
1. wie groß 2. wie alt 3. welche Farbe 4. woher 5. aus welchem Material.
Beispiele: *a large (1) fresh (2) green (3) cabbage*
some small (1) antique (2) Chinese (4) vases

Übungen

1 Put the adjectives in these sentences in the correct order.

a) She was wearing a black short stylish dress.

____

b) We went to an Italian little friendly restaurant.

____

c) There's nothing better on a hot long day than a swim in a clear, beautiful, ice-cold lake! ______________________________

____

d) In the States we stayed in a Colonial charming 200-year-old building that had been converted into a hotel. ______________________________

____

e) I like to start the day with a cup of strong black nice coffee.

____

f) They spent the evening watching Hollywood old scary black and white movies. ______________________________

____

g) My dad still has a 1980s enormous car phone that he keeps in the car as a joke. ______________________________

____

Tipp | Adjektive, die die Größe oder Länge von Gegenständen beschreiben, stehen normalerweise **vor** Adjektiven, die die Breite oder Form beschreiben:
Beispiele: *a tall, fat man; an enormous square birthday cake*

2 Complete the sentences with one of the adjectives below.

blue ▪ delicious ▪ Egyptian ▪ English ▪ gold ▪ long ▪ tall ▪ wooden

a) When I was a little girl I had ________________ blond hair.

b) I love your new ________________ scarf – where did you get it?

c) My grandmother had a small ________________ box where she kept her old love letters.

d) Millions of tourists have visited the ancient ________________ pyramids.

e) Simon gave Justine an expensive ________________ ring.

f) Come and try some of my ________________ freshly-baked cake!

g) She did well to pass that difficult ________________ exam.

h) "Who's that __________ thin boy over there?" "That's my brother!"

3 Match up the two halves of the sentences below.

a) Mick is the man in the old
b) The building has a large
c) She screamed when she saw
d) On holiday she met a handsome
e) Scott has downloaded a really annoying
f) He's the most exciting
g) I found the money in a small

i) the little grey mouse.
ii) brown leather jacket.
iii) striped American flag on the roof.
iv) 15-year-old Spanish boy.
v) young player on the team.
vi) white paper bag.
vii) long ringtone onto his phone.

Fehler-Check

Fill in the gaps with the adjectives in brackets, changing the word order if necessary.

Birmingham is a ____ (English/modern/large) city located in the Midlands. A centre of industry, it was once known for its ________________________________ (dirty/old) factories, where even children – ____________________________________ ________ (young/poor/working-class) children, of course – had to work long hours with ________________________________ (metal/huge) machinery in noisy factory halls. Since then, of course, Birmingham has changed a lot. Today, the city centre is no longer a collection of _________ ________________________ (narrow/dark) streets, but instead is filled with shops and __________________________________ (bright/Italian-style) cafés. Visitors can still see one important feature of industrial Birmingham: the ____ (Victorian/long/water) canals that were used to transport goods around the city and to other parts of the country. These have also been modernised, and tourists can enjoy a __________________________________ (pleasant/three-hour) boat trip through the city's many waterways.

☐ **Fehler**	**0 – 2 Fehler** Super!	**3 – 5 Fehler** In Ordnung!	**mehr als 5 Fehler** Bitte noch einmal üben!

Die Satzstellung von Adverbien

On a weekday, I get up usually at around 7. I have always a ||
hot shower and clean before breakfast my teeth. I don't have ||
always a proper breakfast – I drink sometimes just a coffee. |
But I eat at the weekend a big breakfast with my family: rolls, |
cheese, ham, jam, chocolate spread and lots of tea. We sit |
sometimes for two or three hours around the table ... ||

Regeln

1. Wie für Adjektive gibt es auch für Adverbien (*adverbs*) und adverbiale Bestimmungen (*adverbials*) eine vorgeschriebene Stellung im Satz. *Adverbs of manner* (wie etwas gemacht wird, z. B. *happily*), *adverbials of time* (wann etwas gemacht wird, z. B. *last week*) und *adverbials of place* (wo etwas gemacht wird, z. B. *in the yard*) stehen am Satzende.
   Beispiele: *The children were playing happily.*
   The children were playing in the yard.

2. Bei mehreren Adverbien in einem Satz kommt zuerst *manner*, dann *place*, dann *time*.
   Beispiel: *The children played happily in the garden all afternoon.*

3. *Adverbs of frequency* (wie oft etwas gemacht wird, z. B. *always, sometimes*) werden **vor** dem Hauptverb und **nach** dem Hilfsverb oder einer Form von *be* platziert.
   Beispiele: *I never want to see him again. She's always late.*

4. Achtung: *Adverbials of frequency* (Wortgruppen wie z. B. *twice a year, three times a week*) stehen am Ende des Satzes.
   Beispiel: *You should clean your teeth at least twice a day.*

Übungen

1 Put the following words in the correct order.

a) Italy August go in usually we to

____

b) evening next a party there's Saturday at youth club the

____

c) was dad the singing my shower loudly in

____

d) school week hard at worked last they

____

e) drives he always carefully very

____

f) during is America set the War in film Civil the

____

g) the opens corner on supermarket at the 8 a.m.

____

h) usually summer is weather in the warm

____

Tipp Es ist manchmal möglich, ein *adverb of frequency*, *place* oder *time* an den Anfang statt an das Ende des Satzes zu stellen. Das macht man aber nur, wenn man die Angabe zu Häufigkeit, Ort oder Zeit betonen möchte.
Beispiel: *I usually get up at about 7.30. Sometimes, however, I sleep till 10.*

2 Put the word or phrase in brackets into the following sentences in the correct position.

a) He's been to China. (never)

____

b) The little boy cycled down the road. (slowly)

____

c) The train leaves. (at half past eleven)

____

d) Andy lived for three years. (in England)

____

e) We go out for an Indian meal. (sometimes)

____

f) She thanked us for all our help. (politely)

____

g) They're leaving for Paris. (tomorrow morning)

____

3 Correct any mistakes in word order that you can find in these sentences. One sentence is correct.

a) The team wins often important matches.
b) If we want good seats, we'll have to leave tomorrow early.
c) I'm going tomorrow evening to the cinema – do you want to come too?
d) Lucy works in the school holidays in a flower shop
e) I always enjoy cycling through the woods in my free time.
f) The dog ate in the kitchen hungrily the meat.
g) Claudia never had seen so many homeless people before.
h) My earliest memory is playing when I was three in the garden.

Fehler-Check

Put the adverbs/adverbials in the correct gap in the following sentences.

We ___________ stay ____ ________________________ (in a Swiss mountain hut / in the Christmas holidays / often). Last year it snowed ________________________________ (every day / heavily). It was very cold, and I ____________________ looked forward to returning _______________________________________ (at the end of the day / always / to the hut). We were ________________ greeted by the sight of the wood fire burning ________________________ ___________ (cheerfully / in the fireplace / usually). But we arrived ____ (one evening / at the door of the hut) and found it locked. The owner of the hut ___________ collected wood ______________________________________ ___________, but had not gone out that morning because the wind was blowing so _________________ (once a day / normally / strongly / from the village). All we could do was stand _____________ together __________ _________________ (outside the hut / closely). It was a huge relief when the owner returned ____ (20 minutes later / in his car)!

☐ **Fehler**	**0 – 4 Fehler** Super!	**5 – 10 Fehler** In Ordnung!	**mehr als 10 Fehler** Bitte noch einmal üben!

Present und *past participle clauses*

Having move to London, Shakespeare began to write plays for a theatrical company called the Lord Chamberlain's Men. He also acted in the plays, having work closely with the other actors to produce great dramas, comedies and tragedies. Today, been one of the most important writers in the English language, his plays are still performed all over the world.

Regeln

1. Es gibt im Englischen zwei Partizipien: das *present participle*, das auf *–ing* endet, und das *past participle* (= 3. Verbform), das bei regelmäßigen Verben auf *–ed* endet. Du kannst diese Partizipien dazu benutzen, Sätze zu verkürzen.

2. Wenn du über zwei Handlungen sprichst, die gleichzeitig passieren, kannst du mithilfe des *present participle* den Satz verkürzen oder aus zwei Sätzen einen Satz machen.
   Beispiele: *Harry burnt his hand while he was cooking the dinner.*
   → *Harry burnt his hand cooking the dinner.*
   He walked in. He was smiling. → *He walked in smiling.*

3. Ein Partizip wird oft benutzt, um eine Situation oder Handlung zu erklären. Es steht dann an erster Stelle.
   Beispiel: *I felt hungry, so I made myself a sandwich.*
   → *Feeling hungry, I made myself a sandwich* (Ich tat es, weil ich Hunger hatte).
   I was bored. I switched on the TV.
   → *Being bored, I switched on the TV.* (Ich tat es, weil mir langweilig war).

4. Wenn du über zwei Handlungen sprichst, die nacheinander passieren oder bei denen die eine Handlung schon länger im Gange ist, kannst du den Satz mithilfe des *perfect participle* verkürzen. Du bildest es mit *having + past participle*.
Beispiele: *After she had slept for 12 hours, she felt much better.*
→ *Having slept for 12 hours, she felt much better.*
As he had been speaking French since he was a child, he was able to translate for the exchange students.
→ *Having spoken French since he was a child, he was able to translate for the exchange students.*

Übungen

1 Shorten the following sentences using a present participle.

a) I saw him when he was smoking a cigarette in the park.

____

b) Dad is sitting on the sofa and he is reading the newspaper.

____

c) They met when they were chatting on the same online forum.

____

d) We got lost while we were looking for the new Italian restaurant.

____

e) I felt bored when I was sitting at home with nothing to do.

____

Tipp Verben wie *be, have, know* oder *want* werden meistens nicht in der *–ing*-Form benutzt. Um den Grund für etwas auszudrücken, werden solche Verben aber oft als *present participles* eingesetzt.
Beispiele: *Being clever, he found the exam very easy.*
Not having much time, she took a taxi to the station.

2 Join the following sentences. Start with a participle clause.

a) I felt tired. I decided to stay at home that evening.

___

b) We knew that Mel can't keep a secret. We didn't tell her about the party.

___

c) He didn't have much money. He got a part-time job.

___

d) They are rich. They can afford expensive holidays.

___

e) He didn't want to disturb us. He left quietly.

___

f) She was cold. She turned up the heating.

___

3 Match up the two halves of the sentences below.

a) Having signed up to Facebook,
b) Having lost his job,
c) Not having met for many years,
d) Having sung "Happy Birthday",
e) Having read the book,
f) Not having paid attention,
g) Having walked for nearly 2 hours,
h) Not having flown before,

i) he couldn't answer the question.
ii) they watched Holly blow out the candles.
iii) they were tired and thirsty.
iv) my uncle was nervous about getting on a plane.
v) he decided to go back to college.
vi) she sent friend requests to all her classmates.
vii) I knew how the film would end.
viii) they were surprised that they recognised each other.

4 Choose the correct alternative in the following sentences.

a) Brushing/Having brushed his teeth, Joe went to bed.
b) Never being/Never having been to New York before, they first went to the Statue of Liberty.
c) Being/Having been unemployed, he doesn't have much money.
d) Losing/Having lost my key, I couldn't get into my flat.
e) Looking/Having looked out of the window, she saw a man breaking into her car.
f) Feeling/Having felt happy, Pat started to whistle cheerfully.

Fehler-Check

Fill the gaps with the present or perfect participle of the verbs given.

Marie was sitting in her room, ________________ (study) for her exams. ________________ (fail) the exams the last time, she needed to do well. ________________ (want) to become a doctor, she had applied to several medical schools. ____________ (not/have) much time for her friends because she was working so hard, she often felt a bit lonely. But she explained: "My dream is to work with sick people, ____________ (help) them to get well again. And, ____________ (decide) to make medicine my career, I have to do all I can to make that dream come true. __________ (not/go) out with my friends every weekend, I can save money, too. There's a long way to go, but, ______________ (be) very determined, I know I can make it!"

☐ Fehler	0 – 2 Fehler	3 – 4 Fehler	mehr als 4 Fehler
	Super!	In Ordnung!	Bitte noch einmal üben!

Relativsätze: *defining* oder *non-defining*?

To make some extra cash, I sold a lot of the DVDs, that I used I
to watch when I was younger. Most of them went to a guy, who I
works with my sister. He wanted them for his son, which is ten I
years old. When I was his age I loved watching the DVDs which I
are very funny but now I'd rather watch films, that are thrillers ... II

Regeln

1. Ein Relativsatz *(relative clause)* ist ein Nebensatz, der uns zusätzliche Informationen zu Personen oder Dingen gibt, die im Hauptsatz erwähnt werden.
   Beispiele: *The girl who lives next door is fifteen years old.*
   Here's the book that you were looking for.

2. Man unterscheidet zwischen *defining relative clauses* und *non-defining relative clauses*. Ein *defining relative clause* enthält Informationen, die benötigt werden, um den Hauptsatz zu verstehen. Er steht **ohne Komma** neben dem Hauptsatz.
   Beispiele: *Where is the book that I lent you?*
   She's the actress who starred in the film.

3. Ein *non-defining relative clause* enthält ergänzende Informationen, die man nicht unbedingt braucht. Wenn man ihn weglässt, bleibt der Hauptsatz trotzdem verständlich. *Non-defining relative clauses* werden vom Hauptsatz **mit Kommas** abgetrennt.
   Beispiele: *This book, which was written in 2001, won the Nobel Prize for Literature.*
   That's Leah Stubbs, who starred in the film "Jungle Days".

4. Ein Relativsatz beginnt meist mit einem Relativpronomen: mit *who, that* oder *which*.
   Beispiel: *That's the man who lives next door to us.*

5. Wenn das Relativpronomen in einem *defining relative clause* nicht Subjekt, sondern Objekt ist, kann es weggelassen werden.
   Beispiele: *I got a text from the girl (who) I met on holiday.*
   The city (which) you see on the map is called York.

Übungen

1 Match up the main clauses with the right defining relative clause.

a) Cats are animals	i) who don't eat meat.
b) The Internet is a medium	ii) that has a lot of desert.
c) A nurse is someone	iii) that like chasing mice.
d) Australia is a country	iv) that is popular throughout the world.
e) A stadium is a place	v) that some people consider dangerous.
f) A journalist is a person	vi) who takes care of sick people.
g) Coffee is a drink	vii) where sports are played.
h) Vegetarians are people	viii) who writes newspaper articles.

Tipp | Nicht vergessen: *Who* bezieht sich auf Personen und *which* auf Gegenstände. *That* kann man dagegen für beides verwenden.

2 Put the relative pronouns *(who, that, which)* in the following sentences into brackets if they can be left out.

a) She's wearing a dress that she bought in an online boutique.

b) A "couch potato" is a person who doesn't do much exercise.

c) She's the girl who wanted to become a supermodel.

d) Look at all these books that I have to read for homework!

e) Here are the photos which I took in Madrid.

f) Paul is the only person who I can talk to about this.

g) Paul is the only person who knows about this.

h) Athens is a city which has a lot of historic buildings.

i) Barack Obama is a person who many people admire.

j) A good teacher is someone who has a lot of patience.

3 Combine the following to make sentences with relative clauses.
Example: *Tony is a football coach. He lives next door to me.*
Tony, who lives next door to me, is a football coach.

a) Jack started school last week. He's my nephew.

____

b) The pizza burnt my mouth. It was delicious.

____

c) Louis gave me his bike. He's moved to Canada now.

____

d) This phone doesn't take very good photos. I got it for my birthday.

____

e) Mike has written a book about surfing. He's a journalist.

____

f) The film has been a surprising success. It came out last week.

____

g) Julie's boyfriend has asked her to marry him. She only met him last week.

____

h) The house needed a lot of renovation work. It was very old.

____

Fehler-Check

Correct the mistakes in the use of relative clauses (underlined) that you find in the sentences below. Write the answers in your exercise book.

Some people would say that Livvy Dolan is the kind of girl, who has everything. In the early 1990s when she was only six she worked as a model. Then she started acting. Tom O'Neill, which was a well-known director at the time, cast her in his film "Monday to Thursday". But the film, which made her really famous, was "Stargazer". She played a young girl escapes her violent father by looking for new stars through her neighbour's telescope. However, Livvy, who was very famous by now started to drink and take drugs. She was even arrested by a police officer caught her driving her car along the pavement one evening. A few months later, she crashed the car which had been a present for her 18th birthday into a shop window. But Livvy is the kind of person, who knows how to fight back. She went into rehab and came out six months later to take up her acting career again.

☐ Fehler	**0 – 2 Fehler** Super!	**3 – 5 Fehler** In Ordnung!	**mehr als 5 Fehler** Bitte noch einmal üben!

Kapitel 1: Zeitformen *(tenses)* richtig gebrauchen

Present perfect oder *simple past*?

1 Seite 6

a) Tom went on holiday yesterday. He'll be back next week.
b) Christopher Columbus discovered the American continent in 1492.
c) I haven't eaten all day, so now I'm really hungry.
d) "Would you like something to drink?" "No, thanks. I've just had a can of Coke."
e) I haven't finished my essay yet, so I should really stay in this evening and do it.
f) We have forgotten to invite Lisa to the party, but if we phone her now she might still be able to come.
g) My uncle moved to Australia when I was two years old, and that was the last time I saw him.
h) Have you ever tried inline skating? It's good fun!
i) I tried water-skiing in Greece last year. It was quite tricky!
j) I think someone has stolen my bike! I can't find it anywhere!

2 Seite 7

a) Fiona has passed all her exams so far this year.
b) Have you ever won a competition?
c) My parents moved here in 1998 and have lived in the same house ever since.
d) I've done my homework, so I can spend the rest of the evening watching TV!
e) "Have you seen Alan lately?" "Yes, I met him in town last week. He says hello!"
f) How many times has Patrick missed the maths lesson this week? He's going to get into trouble!
g) Mr O'Connor has shaved off his beard. He looks completely different now!
h) "Is Jack still there?" "No, he left about 10 minutes ago."
i) Helen has broken her arm so she can't play volleyball for the next six weeks.
j) Our ice hockey team lost our last game, so we need to do better the next time.
k) I have to stay in bed today. I've caught a cold.

3 Seite 8

a) I didn't see Joanne at the party last night.
b) ✓
c) We haven't taken the exam yet – it's not until next week.
d) While Cindy was studying in the USA last year, she kept in touch with her family via Skype.
e) Have you already finished tidying your room? That was quick!
f) ✓

g) "What time did Bill leave?" "At 9 o'clock this morning."

h) ✓

i) I've been here since 4 o'clock waiting for you! Why are you so late?

j) This book was written in 1890, but it's still interesting to read today.

Seite 9

4 a) "My sister's just had a baby!" "Please give her my love!"

b) Frank arrived at 10 o'clock last night.

c) Have you prepared your presentation yet?

d) Tim left school in 2008.

e) Most people have never won any money in the lottery.

f) Five hundred years ago this region was just one big forest.

g) I've already handed in my essay, so it's too late to change anything now.

h) How many texts have you sent so far this week?

i) They've been in contact through an Internet chatroom for several months now, but they've never met in person.

j) My alarm clock rang at half-past six this morning.

k) Have you ever been to a rock festival?

l) I haven't spent so much time on my social networking pages recently, and I find I don't really miss it.

m) Two months ago, nobody knew his name; now he's famous!

Seite 10

Fehler-Check

When Jana Müller's parents first told her they were moving to Australia for three years, she didn't know whether to be happy or sad. That was six months ago, and since then Jana has adapted to life "down under" and has learned/learnt to love the Aussie way of life. "I've already made lots of new friends. So far I've visited two of the great cities, Sydney and Melbourne, although we haven't had time to go to Adelaide yet. And my parents have booked a trip to the Great Barrier Reef for this year – I can't wait!"

At first Jana didn't speak the language very well, but her English has now improved and she has even started to speak with an Australian accent! And what does she miss most about Germany? "Real pretzels! But I have just discovered a shop near here run by a German couple who came to live here in 1990 and who bake traditional German bread. The taste reminds me of home!"

Present perfect progressive

1 a) The children have been running around all afternoon, so they must be tired now.
b) I have been searching for the information I need on the Internet, but I haven't found it yet.
c) This term we have been reading Shakespeare's "Macbeth" in our English class. It isn't always easy to understand!
d) "Why are you crying?" "I have been cutting onions!"
e) It has been snowing for several hours now and the roads are very slippery, so please drive carefully!
f) Holly has been saving her pocket money to buy tickets to the Pink concert.
g) I have been feeling sick all day. I think I'll go to bed early.
h) My cousin has been travelling around South America for the past three months, but he's coming home next week.
i) "What have you been doing today?" "Oh, nothing much."

Seite 12

2 a) Gracie has been staying with us since last Friday.
b) I have been reading a good book this week.
c) We have been listening to the radio for two hours.
d) The sun has been shining all day.
e) They have been swimming since lunchtime.
f) My foot has been hurting since I fell over.

Seite 13

3 a) How often have you listened to that CD?
b) How long have you been playing the guitar? You're really good!
c) I've left a message for Tina three times this week, but she hasn't answered me yet.
d) How often has he asked you to dance?
e) She has been drinking coffee all afternoon – she won't be able to sleep tonight!

Fehler-Check

Seite 14

Now we go live to Matt Shea for his report on the German team.
"The Germans have been training hard all year and are ready for the challenge of this championship. The team has been playing well so far but the players know that the next match won't be easy. They have been staying at the hotel behind me

since last Friday and have been relaxing today after their match against Serbia. I asked their new captain what he has been doing since then.
'Not much, really! I have been watching a bit of TV and listening to my MP3 player. Some of the other players have been working out in the gym, and others have been phoning friends and family back home. We have been looking at some videos of the next team we have to play against, too.' The team's coach, with the help of his assistants, has been doing all he can to make sure that the team is motivated for the next match. So let's wish them good luck and say: go Germany!"

Past perfect

Seite 16

1 a) By the time we got to the party, they had drunk all the lemonade.
b) Charlie was very tired because he hadn't slept well.
c) I got really sunburnt at the weekend because I had sat in the garden too long.
d) When we got home, we realised we had forgotten our key.
e) Poppy was upset because Leo hadn't spoken to her all week.
f) We thought our cat had run away, but we found it again in our neighbour's garden.
g) Julia had written half of her essay when her computer broke down.
h) I couldn't buy the new CD I wanted because I had spent all my pocket money.
i) The team went out to celebrate after they had won the match.
j) Chris wrote to thank us because we had given him a present.
k) Anna sent us copies of the photos she had taken.
l) After we had bought the ice-cream, we sat down under a tree to eat it.

Seite 17

2 a) My parents went to Spain in May – they had won the holiday in a competition.
b) After the rain had stopped, we continued our walk.
c) I decided not to see the film after Jake had told me the ending.
d) We were sorry when David and Cathy moved away: they had lived next door to us for many years.
e) Emily had burnt the dinner, so we ordered a pizza.
f) Everyone was surprised when the team won. They hadn't won a match for months.
g) When Columbus discovered America, he didn't know that the Vikings had been there before him.
h) Zoe had to stay late at school because she had broken one of the rules.
i) We didn't want any dessert because we had already had so much to eat.

j) Daniel didn't know about Lily's new boyfriend because nobody had told him.
k) She didn't meet you because you had left the party when she arrived.

Seite 18

3 b) Pete borrowed my book because he had lost his.
c) Jane wasn't hungry because she had eaten a big lunch.
d) Gary was tired because he had run 15 kilometres.
e) I got into trouble because I hadn't done my homework.
f) The house was very dirty because they had had a party.
g) The tree was lying on the ground because it had fallen down during a storm.
h) Kyra felt depressed because Rob had broken up with her.
i) Lucy was late because she had forgotten to set her alarm clock.
j) Paul was very happy because he had won a prize.

Seite 19

4 a) Billy walked home because he had missed the bus.
b) I hadn't checked my messages, so I didn't know what time we were meeting.
c) Max hadn't visited Berlin before, so he wanted to see all the historic sites.
d) Stella was angry that Alex had posted the story on the Internet.
e) Josh hadn't baked a cake before, but it tasted really good!

5 a) Mein Vater wurde geboren, nachdem meine Großeltern nach Kanada ausgewandert/umgezogen waren.
b) Ben war müde, nachdem er 10 Kilometer gelaufen war.
c) Es gab keine Milch mehr, weil Eva alles ausgetrunken hatte.
d) Nachdem die letzte Band gespielt hatte, gingen alle nach Hause.

Fehler-Check

Seite 20

Seventeen-year-old Tamara Haworth was last year's winner of “A Talent for Singing”. Now, one year later, she talks about her experience of winning.
“I had sung in lots of competitions before I entered “A Talent for Singing”, but that was my first casting show. The hardest part of winning was becoming a celebrity overnight. Joey Cramer, who had won the show one year before me, gave me some good advice: “Never forget who your real friends are.” This is very important! Just after the show ended, a lot of girls at my school who had never spoken to me before suddenly said they were my ‘friend’. Some of them even told newspapers about things I had done; unfortunately, a lot of these stories were not true. One paper even printed a story about me and a well-known rapper – I had never met

the guy! At that point, I really found out who my true friends are, friends I had made before I became famous and who I can still have a laugh with today."

Future forms I: will oder *going to?*

Seite 22

1. a) People will live on the moon.
   b) Cars will run on electricity instead of petrol.
   c) Everybody will grow their own fruit and vegetables.
   d) Nobody will eat meat.
   e) Schools will have virtual teachers.
   f) Mobile phones will be 10 times smaller than they are now.
   g) A lot more people will work from home.
   h) It will take three hours to fly to Australia from Europe.
   i) We will build our houses of recycled material.

Seite 23

2. a) Ich werde ein Bad nehmen, wenn ich zu Hause bin.
   b) Wir werden uns nach der Schule mit Harry treffen.
   c) Ich will eines Tages nach New York fahren.
   d) Ich werde dir bei dem Projekt helfen.
   e) Er will Gitarre spielen.

Seite 24

3. a) On Tuesday Ryan's going to have a driving lesson after school.
   b) On Wednesday he's going to hand in an article for the school magazine.
   c) On Thursday he's going to help plan the youth club summer party.
   d) On Friday he's going to buy a present for his grandma.
   e) On Saturday he's going to go to his grandma's 70th birthday party.
   f) On Sunday at 10 a. m. he's going to meet Helen at the swimming pool.

Seite 25

4. a) He's going to win the race.
   b) The concert is going to begin.
   c) They're going to have a barbecue.
   d) She's going to bake a cake.
   e) They're going to kiss.

5. a) Adam's Halloween party is in two weeks, but I already know what I'm going to wear.
   b) Sorry, I can't talk now. I'll call you back later.
   c) I don't think Luis will come this evening – he doesn't really like the theatre.

d) We're going to go swimming this afternoon – would you like to come?
e) Mark is going to ask Amy out! I wonder what she'll say!
f) Maybe he'll let you borrow his laptop – why don't you ask him?
g) "Can I take your order?" "Um, OK, I'll have the chicken, please."

Fehler-Check Seite 26

Ten years from now – what will your life be like?
"I think I'll enjoy my life more in ten years than I do now", says Greg, 17. "I won't be at school any more and I'm sure I'll have a good job. I'm going to study to be a computer programmer, because then I'll be able to earn lots of money. My specialisation: I'm going to design computer games!"
Sonya, on the other hand, is not so positive about the future. "I think a lot of things will change in the next ten years, but not always for the better. The level of pollution in our cities will rise and, as a result, the quality of life will fall. That's why I am not going to stay in London. As soon as I have enough money, I'm going to move to the countryside. I'm going to sell my car and go everywhere by bike. And I'm going to run my own vegetarian restaurant. People will have to start changing the way they live if our planet is going to survive."

Future forms II: present tenses, future perfect

1. a) We're planning a surprise party for Melanie next weekend. Seite 28
   b) I'm going to the dentist's on Thursday.
   c) My parents are driving to Scotland in the morning.
   d) What are you doing tomorrow?
   e) I'm having dinner with my boyfriend's family this evening.

2. a) FALSE: "Shape up for summer" finishes at half past six in the evening. Seite 29
   b) TRUE
   c) FALSE: Football for the under-10s starts on the first day of the month.
   d) FALSE: Football training finishes late on Wednesday.
   e) FALSE: The five-a-side tournament starts before lunch.
   f) FALSE: The early morning running group meets twice a week.

3. a) Eve is flying to Portugal next week.
   b) The course begins at exactly 9 a. m. – please be on time.
   c) We are studying for our French test at Lena's house after school tomorrow.

d) When does the last bus leave for the city centre?
e) Eddie finishes his training on 31st July.
f) Fantastic news – Alison and Matt are getting married in autumn!
g) The project doesn't start until the end of the year.

Seite 30

4 a) I'm playing football with my friends next Saturday.
b) I'm sure Philip will win the match tomorrow – he's the best player.
c) The new museum opens next week, and everyone in my class is going.
d) "Mum, can I stay up and watch the film?" "No, it finishes too late."
e) I'm having my hair cut tomorrow – really short!
f) Do you know what Claire is doing this weekend?
g) I'll drive home if you're too tired.
h) The concert starts at eight o'clock.
i) Selina is moving in with her boyfriend as soon as he has found a new flat.
j) George is meeting his old English teacher next Wednesday.

Seite 31

5 a) By the time he's 19, he'll have had his first hit single.
b) By the time he's 22, he'll have started his own business.
c) By the time he's 25, he'll have made his first million euros.
d) By the time he's 28, he'll have written a best-selling novel.
e) By the time he's 30, he'll have bought a penthouse in L.A.
f) By the time he's 33, he'll have moved to a small island.

6 a) No, I won't be at home at 9 o'clock. I'll have left the house by then.
b) If we don't hurry up, they'll have eaten all the cake by the time we get to the party!
c) Next December my parents will have known each other for 25 years.
d) By the end of the summer holidays, thousands of tourists will have visited the castle.
e) By this time next week we'll have taken our exams.

Seite 32

Fehler-Check

Next term I'm going to a school in England for three weeks. My head teacher has given me permission to go because I'm not taking any exams next term. While I'm in England, I'm staying with a guest family. We've been e-mailing each other for the past few weeks: they told me they will have painted the guest room by the time I arrive, just for me! As well as this, they're taking me on daytrips at the weekends,

which is great. One attraction I really want to see is the new Roman Museum in York – it opens in a few weeks from now.
By the time I leave, I hope I'll have made some new friends and that I'll have enjoyed the experience!

Zeitformen in der indirekten Rede

1 a) She said (that) Marcus played the drums in a band. Seite 34
b) He told me (that) he had learned to ski the year before.
c) He said (that) he had never eaten sushi.
d) She told me (that) William was studying to be a doctor.
e) Ella said (that) she would lend me her book.
f) Liam told me (that) his parents were going to buy a new car.
g) She said (that) she could swim underwater.
h) Our teacher told us/me (that) we/I had to come on time.
i) He said (that) he might win first prize.

2 a) They said they were celebrating their exam results with a party that evening. Seite 35
b) Daniel said he'd meet me back there later that afternoon.
c) She told him that he couldn't go with them.
d) He asked me to send him the information by the following week at the latest.
e) Susannah said that her grandpa had been upset because she'd forgotten to send him a birthday card.

3 a) Alan told us what he'd done on his holiday. Seite 36
b) My teacher told my parents that I'd been late every day that week.
c) My teacher said my parents had to come and see her.
d) Jessica said Sean had cheated on her.
e) Jessica told Sean she had cheated on him.

4 a) "But he told me he couldn't ride a bike."
b) "But he told me he would be at home this weekend."
c) "But he told me he loved playing tennis."
d) "But he told me he had got two cats."
e) "But he told me he was going to Spain in July."

5 a) I asked Jacob where he lived. Seite 37
b) I asked him whether he'd still got his dog.

c) I asked him what he had been doing in the last few years.
d) I asked him if he had seen any of our other old friends recently.
e) I asked him how his sister was.
f) I asked him if he had ever gone on his round-the-world trip.
g) I asked him when he would next be in town.
h) I asked him if he could send me his e-mail address.

Seite 38

Fehler-Check

I asked my grandmother what she remembered best about her childhood. She told me she could remember playing in the streets. She thought the world had been a much safer place back then and that children's parents had given them much more freedom than children had now. I then asked her if/whether she missed the "good old days". She replied that she preferred living in the 21st century. She said that later on that day she was going to chat online to her brother in Australia. It wouldn't cost her a penny and she would be able to see him at the same time.

Kapitel 2: Verben: Typische Hürden

Conditionals

Seite 40

1. a) If I lived in France, I'd have to speak French.
b) If we went camping, we'd sleep in a tent.
c) If the teacher saw me sending texts in class, she'd take my phone away.
d) If we visited Los Angeles, we might see some film stars.
e) If Katie didn't waste so much time, she'd finish her work much faster.
f) If my parents let me stay out late, we could all go to the disco.
g) If I were you, I wouldn't eat so much chocolate.
h) If people were more friendly, the world would be a better place.
i) If the weather was hotter, we could go for a swim in the lake.
j) If I won an Oscar, I'd be very proud of myself.

2. a) If I had time, I'd learn another language.
b) We'd invite Lindsay to the party if she was in town.
c) If he loved me, he'd phone.
d) If you had a dog, you'd have to take it for walks every day.
e) If I lived by the sea, I'd swim every morning.

f) I think you'd enjoy the film if you saw it.
g) We'd go to the concert if the tickets weren't so expensive.
h) If Colin did more exercise, he'd lose some weight.
i) Jenny would visit Mexico if she spoke Spanish.
j) If my parents found out about the party, they'd make me stay at home for a month!

Seite 42

3 a) If I were the Chancellor of Germany, I'd make things better for young people.
b) A lot of the rainforest will disappear if we don't do more to protect it.
c) If Trisha goes to the party too, I won't speak to her.
d) If I could travel through time, I'd visit New York in the early 19th century.
e) The city centre would be much cleaner if cars weren't allowed to drive there.
f) If you want to phone me later, I'll be home after 4 o'clock.
g) It would be a real surprise if New Zealand won the next World Cup!
h) If you take some nice photos while you're on holiday, will you send me some copies?
i) If you don't start writing that essay soon, it won't be finished on time.
j) What would you change about your school if you were head teacher for a day?
k) If you join a sports club, you will make lots of new friends.
l) If I had the chance, I would marry Paris Hilton.

Seite 43

4 a) If my parents had had enough money, they would have moved to a bigger house.
b) If he hadn't got in trouble with the police, he would not have run away.
c) If I had liked the dress, I'd have bought it.
d) The accident would not have happened if he'd been more careful.
e) If I had stayed on at school, I might have better qualifications now.

5 a) If we had taken a map with us, we wouldn't have got lost.
b) If the shop had had the shoes in my size, I would have bought them.
c) If my sister hadn't helped me revise, I wouldn't have passed my exam.
d) If Theresa hadn't been ill, she would have come out with us.
e) If Ben had had enough money for a taxi, he wouldn't have had to walk home.
f) If I hadn't thought the book was boring, I'd have finished reading it.
g) If Charlotte hadn't forgotten to set her alarm clock, she would have woken up on time.
h) If the oil tanker hadn't crashed, thousands of animals wouldn't have died.

Lösungen

Seite 45

6 a) had; b) had; c) would; d) had; e) would – had

7 a) What would you do if you found a lot of money on the street?
b) If I had never met Rhonda, my life would have been very different.
c) If he'd/he had had a part-time job in the school holidays, he might have been able to come on holiday with us.
d) ✓

Seite 46

Fehler-Check

This week we talk to three of our readers about moments that changed their lives, and how things would have been different if they had made different choices.
Emma: "If I hadn't moved to London when I was 18, I wouldn't have met Ian and we wouldn't have got married. Also, I'm sure I wouldn't have my own business now if I still lived in the village where I grew up!"
Chris: "If I hadn't become a professional tennis player, I wouldn't have travelled around the world. And if I had continued to play, I might have won a Grand Slam tournament! Now I'm a tennis coach, and if I trained someone to win a big tournament, I would celebrate big time!"
Brian: "If my first book had been a best-seller, I wouldn't have learned that you have to work for success. Now I know that even if I wrote a novel that nobody liked, I could forget it and start again the next day. I wouldn't take it personally."

Passive voice

Seite 48

1 a) These rooms are cleaned once a week.
b) This photo was taken in Hamburg.
c) The match is being played tomorrow.
d) A new president will be elected next month.
e) My bike has been stolen.
f) The new road is going to be finished soon.
g) The door had not been locked.
h) The new Spielberg film is being shown next week.
i) This vase has been broken.
j) The computer was repaired very quickly.

Seite 49

2 a) "Macbeth" was written by Shakespeare.
b) Paper was invented by the Chinese.

c) The Gulf War was fought against Iraq.
d) Australia was discovered by Captain Cook.
e) Snakes are eaten in Indonesia.
f) The 2010 World Cup was won by Spain.
g) The Pyramids were built by the Ancient Egyptians.
h) Many American TV series are filmed in Hollywood.
i) Easter is celebrated by Christians around the world.
j) The 2012 Olympic Games are being held in London.

3 a) The church was built in the 16th century. Seite 50
b) The money had been hidden in the cellar.
c) You will be given the information soon.
d) All the letters have been sent.
e) The roof had been damaged in the storm.
f) These cars were made in Japan.
g) The film premiere is being held in Berlin.
h) Your books will be delivered next week.

4 a) In what part of the world is rice grown? Seite 51
b) Mozart was born in 1756.
c) The factory will be closed down next month.
d) Vicky should be given the first prize for her painting.
e) The papers haven't been signed yet.
f) The thieves got into the building because the door hadn't been locked.
g) How many languages are spoken in South Africa?

Fehler-Check

Seite 52

A man has been arrested for stealing jewels.
He was seen running away from a jeweller's shop that had been robbed a few minutes before.
The jewels that were taken were worth a lot of money.
The man is now being questioned by the police about this and other recent jewel robberies.
His house will also be searched.
He could be sent to prison for up to 5 years.

Lösungen

Gerund

Seite 54

1. a) Drinking coffee for breakfast helps me wake up in the morning.
   b) Baking your own cookies is a lot of fun.
   c) I don't really enjoy sleeping in a tent.
   d) Sending messages is so easy nowadays – all you need is a mobile phone.
   e) Taking a walk in the fresh air will help you to concentrate better.
   f) I've always loved teaching, which is why I'm planning to go to Haiti and work in a school there.
   g) Starting a new job can be quite frightening at first.
   h) If you've finished eating, put your plate in the dishwasher.

Seite 55

2. a) losing; b) shopping; c) clapping; d) lying; e) winning; f) forgetting; g) sitting; h) choosing; i) agreeing

3. a) Winning the gold medal was the highlight of her sporting career.
   b) When we heard the loud clapping, we knew that the concert had finished.
   c) Choosing the right place to go on holiday isn't easy.
   d) Leo got into trouble for losing the keys.
   e) Lying in the sun all day is not a good idea – you'll get sunburnt!
   f) I don't like forgetting people's birthdays – that's why I always write them down.
   g) She prefers sitting next to the window on planes.
   h) I don't remember agreeing to go with you!
   i) Shopping online isn't as much fun as going into town with your friends.

Seite 56

4. a) + iv) b) + viii) c) + vi) d) + vii)
   e) + ix) f) + v) g) + ii) h) + x)
   i) + i) j) + iii)

Seite 57

5. a) I know that Jodie's got the CD – I remember giving it to her last week.
   b) Did you remember to call Thomas to tell him what time we're meeting?
   c) Why don't you try asking at your local library?
   d) He tried several times to contact Erica but she never answered her phone.
   e) We stopped to talk to a friend on the way to the station and nearly missed our train.
   f) Please stop talking – I can't hear what she's saying.

Fehler-Check

Seite 58

Saturday. Very tired, so getting up wasn't easy, but I don't like being late on days like this. And it was a big day: our demonstration in the city centre! Showing the government that they must do more to protect the environment is really important, I believe. I even remembered to take my huge "Green World" flag along. The organisers were interested in seeing if any local politicians would turn up. Several members of the Green Party were there, of course, but some of the others seemed to be afraid of meeting the demonstrators and listening to their concerns – typical! Marching through the city was great, as we got lots of media attention. We even stopped to hand in a petition at the parliament building. A long day – looking forward to having a nice long sleep tomorrow morning.
Sunday. I normally love lying for hours in bed, but today...

Phrasal verbs

Seite 60

1 a) Richard got up so late this morning that he didn't even come to school.
b) Nice to see you again! Please come in!
c) Can you pay for my coffee? I've left my purse at home.
d) Maddie doesn't want to go out with us this evening.
e) I'm tired of waiting for Alison. Let's just go without her.
f) Please slow down! The speed limit here is only 30 kilometres an hour.
g) Try on these trousers. I'll buy them for you if they fit.
h) She grew up in a small village in the heart of the English countryside.
i) Our car broke down on the motorway last weekend.
j) I was so happy when Eric asked for my phone number!
k) "How did you break your arm?" "I fell off a wall."
l) They set out just after breakfast and arrived at lunchtime.

Seite 61

2 a) Take off your jacket and have a seat.
b) I need to take my books back to the library.
c) Darren is going out with Michelle.
d) Is Ava here? I need to talk to her.
e) Please fill in this form and return it by Friday.
f) When is Mary coming back from her holiday?
g) If you write it down, it'll help you remember it.
h) Would you like to come round this evening? We could get a pizza.

Lösungen

i) I've been feeling a lot more relaxed since I took up yoga.

j) Watch out! You nearly stepped on my foot!

Seite 61

❸ a) + iii) b) + viii) c) + vi) d) + x)
e) + ii) f) + ix) g) + iv) h) + i)
i) + vii) j) + v)

Seite 62

❹ a) My brother woke me up playing loud music first thing this morning.

b) I've finished with this now – you can take it away.

c) ✓

d) This heater's very hot – can you turn it down, please?

e) Ray arrives at 6 o'clock this evening, so I'll be able to pick him up after work.

f) Ginny didn't do her homework, so the teacher told her off.

g) The tree is too big now – we'll have to cut it down.

Seite 63

❺ a) come – came; b) putting – put; c) got – get; d) going – going; e) take – took; f) give – gave; g) looking – looked

Seite 64

Fehler-Check

a) Check in your bags at the check-in desk.

b) Go through passport control and the security check.

c) Your hand luggage is put through the x-ray machine.

d) You get your hand luggage back on the other side of the machine.

e) Sit down in the departure lounge until your flight is called.

f) Get on the plane and find your seat.

g) Sit down and fasten your seatbelt.

h) Listen to the safety instructions.

i) The plane takes off.

j) Get off the plane.

k) Go through passport control again.

l) Pick up your suitcases at baggage claim.

m) Go out of the airport and enjoy your holiday!

Used to oder *be used to*?

Seite 66

❶ a) My father used to smoke, but he gave up about 10 years ago.

b) Charlie used to run more than 20 kilometres a week until he injured his knee.

c) "Where did you use to go to school?" "Knoxfield High School."

d) I didn't use to like olives, but now I eat them all the time!
e) People used to write a lot of letters before e-mail was invented.
f) "Did you use to live in Berlin?" "No, in Dresden."

Seite 67

2 a) It was difficult in the big city at first, but now I am used to living there.
b) I used to play the piano, but I don't really have time nowadays.
c) "I hope you don't mind our dog." "No, it's OK – I am used to animals."
d) Susie used to be my best friend when we were at school.
e) The new computer program was easy to follow, so we got used to working with it very quickly.
f) It isn't easy to get used to living in a completely different culture.
g) Jimmy has really changed: he didn't use to be so arrogant.
h) I didn't use to enjoy reading until I discovered the "Harry Potter" series.
i) When you start your new school you'll have to get used to doing lots of homework every evening.

3 a) Did you use to be a Justin Bieber fan, too?
b) Elena is used to speaking Italian – she goes to Italy every summer.
c) Anyone who lives in Britain is used to rain!
d) I didn't use to eat vegetables when I was a child.
e) He used to be a famous movie star, but now nobody remembers his name.
f) Her family returned from South Africa because they couldn't get used to the climate.

Fehler-Check

Seite 68

The secret of my success: athletics champion Angie Collins

"Even when I was very young, I used to love running and jumping, and I found out that I had a natural talent for athletics. From the age of 8, I used to train every weekend, although I didn't use to think of it like that: as far as I was concerned, I was just having fun. Nobody was more surprised than me when I won my first junior title, but then I started to get used to being a winner and I realised I loved that feeling. At first, that was what used to motivate me, but not any more. Now that I take part in several competitions a year, I'm used to winning just some of the time. Nowadays, I try to be a role model, too. I go and talk to young people about how important it is to get used to taking regular exercise from a young age. It's great when someone tells me they didn't use to do any sport at all until I inspired them to start exercising!"

L

Lösungen

Kapitel 3: Häufige Fehler rund ums Nomen

Countable und *uncountable nouns*

Seite 70

1. a) + iv) b) + viii) c) + vi) d) + x)
e) + vii) f) + iii) g) + ix) h) + i)
i) + v) j) + ii)

2. a) David doesn't like television. He never watches it.
b) What terrible weather! It hasn't stopped raining all day.
c) I'm hungry. I'm going to make myself a sandwich.
d) We could hear lovely music coming from an open window.
e) No, I don't eat meat. I'm a vegetarian.
f) It's really cold today. Put on a jacket before you go out.
g) It took Annie a long time to find work after she left school.
h) We saw an interesting film about space travel last week.
i) Jane has had an accident! She's broken her arm.
j) Cheese can be made from cows' milk or goats' milk.

Seite 71

3. a) Do you drink coffee? I don't.
b) Would you like a coffee? Fiona's just gone to make one.
c) "We're going on holiday tomorrow." "Have a good time!"
d) Sorry, I won't have time to help you. I've got too much homework.
e) Walking on the Great Wall of China was an amazing experience.
f) You really need experience to do this job well.
g) Here's a glass. The drinks are in the kitchen – help yourself!
h) The church windows are made of special coloured glass.
i) My sister's got long blond hair.
j) The Internet helps people to get important information.
k) The chairs are made of wood.

Seite 72

4. a) Hurry up! We don't have much time.
b) The news isn't good. Thousands of animals have died in the forest fire.
c) I need some information about working abroad.
d) You'll have to ask for permission before you use this equipment.
e) There are too many new words to learn – I'll never remember all of them.
f) By the end of the holiday, they only had a little money left.

g) I lost my purse while I was out shopping, but I found it again before it got stolen. That was a real piece of luck!

h) Does this machine use much electricity?

i) Can I give you some advice? It's not a good idea to hang out with Gary and his friends.

j) If we hung a few pictures on the wall, this room would look much nicer.

k) When there is a lot of rain, our local river sometimes floods.

5 a) "Is your brother still looking for work for the school holidays?" "No, he's got a job now in our local supermarket." Seite 73

b) My parents like old furniture. They have a table from the 18th century.

c) There used to be heavy traffic in our town, but now cars have been banned from the centre.

d) Have you got enough light to read your book? Why don't you switch on a lamp?

e) I've always loved music. I've even started writing songs myself, but I only sing them when I'm alone!

f) We had beautiful weather for our picnic – it was a sunny day.

Fehler-Check

Seite 74

Suzie writes: I really need a piece of advice. Everybody says I am really good at music and I'd love to take part in a casting show. The problem is my parents, who say I'm too young (I'm 15). I sent off for all the information, and I discovered I need permission from my parents to audition. They don't listen when I tell them this is a dream of mine. Please help!

Kay answers: Sorry, but the bad news is: I agree with your parents. A career in the music business is hard work. Even if you are very musical, you also need luck to become really successful, and you must be tough, which isn't easy for a teenager. You say you have talent; well, that won't disappear in the next few years. Work on your music, but get an education, too. Then you'll still be able to get a job if, like most people, you don't instantly have a number one hit!

Pair nouns und andere Ausnahmen

1 a) We all dressed up as ballet dancers for Carnival – we even wore bright pink tights! Seite 76

b) A shirt, a skirt, a pair of tights and smart, high-heeled boots: the perfect autumn outfit.

c) I think I need a new pair of glasses – I can hardly see a thing!

d) She got her first glasses when she was only 7 years old and, like most children, didn't really enjoy wearing them.

e) These shorts are perfect for a hot summer day.

f) I need a pair of scissors to cut out this picture.

g) Be careful with those scissors – they're very sharp.

h) Oh no! My trousers have got a hole in the knee!

Seite 77

2 a) My granny wasn't very happy when I wore old dirty jeans/an old dirty pair of jeans/a pair of old dirty jeans to her birthday party.

b) Don't panic – the police are on their way!

c) Those trousers don't/That pair of trousers doesn't go with that orange shirt.

d) Pass me the scissors, please.

e) There are too many people in this room. I'm going outside for some fresh air.

f) Nobody recognised him at first as he was wearing glasses/a pair of glasses.

g) I once had a pair of pyjamas with a big pink rabbit on the front!

3 a) The police are still looking for the jewel thieves.

b) This is a very rare species of bird.

c) That was a very expensive pair of jeans in that shop.

d) Scissors are dangerous for small children, so they should always be kept in a safe place.

e) There are many means of transport in China, but bikes are one of the most popular.

f) The new series is on late at night because it's very violent.

Seite 78

Fehler-Check

Summer camp rules:

* You should bring 2 pairs of waterproof trousers
* Bring some shorts, but also long trousers in case the weather turns cool
* Jeans are good for wearing on hikes, as they are thick and will protect your legs from cuts and scratches
* The nights can be cold, so pack some warm pyjamas to wear inside your sleeping bag
* Don't forget sunscreen and sunglasses
* You may bring a pair of nail scissors; knives are not permitted
* No more than 10 people are allowed to be in a tent at any one time

* The best means of communication with your family is a cell phone, although you will only be allowed to use it at certain times
* Do bring a pair of binoculars for observing birds and other wildlife

Kapitel 4: Reflexivpronomen: Die häufigsten Fehler

Seite 80

1 a) I = myself
b) you = yourself
c) he = himself
d) she = herself
e) it = itself
f) we = ourselves
g) you (plural) = yourselves
h) they = themselves

2 a) If you're thirsty, get yourself a glass of water.
b) Emma burnt herself when she picked up the hot dish.
c) The children went upstairs, washed themselves and cleaned their teeth.
d) I wrote myself a note so that I wouldn't forget to phone Dan.
e) We took a photo of ourselves at Buckingham Palace using the self-timer on our camera.
f) You should all be very proud of yourselves – you've done a great job!
g) The town has made itself famous by selling its locally made ice-cream throughout the country.
h) I painted a picture of myself – it's a self-portrait.
i) Patrick made a video of himself singing and playing the guitar, and uploaded it onto the Internet.

Seite 81

3 a) + iv) b) + viii) c) + vi) d) + i)
e) + ix) f) + x) g) + iii) h) + vii)
i) + ii) j) + v)

Seite 82

4 a) Terri likes Jo, and Jo likes Terri. They like each other.
b) Mia and Ryan have split up and now they're not even talking to each other.
c) In my family we all give each other presents at Christmas.
d) We went into the kitchen to make ourselves something to eat.

e) They met again after nearly 40 years, but in all that time they never forgot each other.

f) My mother phones her brother in Canada once a month and they tell each other all their news.

g) We hated each other when we first met, but now we're best friends.

h) My sister and I have no secrets – we tell each other everything.

i) Romeo and Juliet killed themselves because they loved each other so much.

j) The food was placed on the table in large bowls and everybody helped themselves.

Seite 83

5 a) Where shall we meet? At the bus stop?

b) I like to have a shower every morning.

c) Sean isn't coming with us because he doesn't feel well.

d) I haven't seen my cousin for years, but we always send each other a birthday card.

e) She decorated the whole living room by herself.

f) Have a great holiday – I'll see you when you get back!

g) I could concentrate better if you stopped playing that loud music.

h) I'm just going to comb my hair and then I'll be ready to go.

i) The children need to wash their hands before we eat.

j) She's old enough to dress herself now.

Seite 84

Fehler-Check

My great-grandmother grew up as one of 12 children. She had to do a lot of things by herself, such as dress herself, from a young age. Her father was a baker, who worked for himself in his own shop. Her mother worked too, so the older children had to stay at home and play with each other until she finished work. "Because my parents didn't have much time, I became very independent. I taught myself to cook and sew, and made a lot of my clothes myself. One day my friend Jenny said: 'Why don't you buy yourself a sewing machine? Then you could make enough clothes to sell. We could even start our own company!' I would never have thought of that myself, but Jenny and I had known each other for many years then, and we trusted each other. So that's how our clothing company got started – unusual for the time, as women didn't often run businesses themselves back then. We never became millionaires, but we were quite successful and very proud of ourselves for what we'd achieved!"

Kapitel 5: Fehlerquelle Adjektiv und Adverb

Die Satzstellung von Adjektiven

Seite 86

1. a) She was wearing a stylish short black dress.
   b) We went to a friendly little Italian restaurant.
   c) There's nothing better on a long hot day than a swim in a beautiful, clear, ice-cold lake!
   d) In the States we stayed in a charming 200-year-old Colonial building that had been converted into a hotel.
   e) I like to start the day with a cup of nice strong black coffee.
   f) They spent the evening watching scary old black and white Hollywood movies.
   g) My dad still has an enormous 1980s car phone that he keeps in the car as a joke.

Seite 87

2. a) When I was a little girl I had long blond hair.
   b) I love your new blue scarf – where did you get it?
   c) My grandmother had a small wooden box where she kept her old love letters.
   d) Millions of tourists have visited the ancient Egyptian pyramids.
   e) Simon gave Justine an expensive gold ring.
   f) Come and try some of my delicious, freshly-baked cake!
   g) She did well to pass that difficult English exam.
   h) "Who's that tall thin boy over there?" "That's my brother!"

3. a) + ii) b) + iii) c) + i) d) + iv)
   e) + vii) f) + v) g) + vi)

Fehler-Check

Seite 88

Birmingham is a large modern English city located in the Midlands. A centre of industry, it was once known for its old dirty factories, where even children – poor, young working-class children, of course – had to work long hours with huge metal machinery in noisy factory halls. Since then, of course, Birmingham has changed a lot. Today, the city centre is no longer a collection of dark narrow streets, but instead is filled with shops and bright Italian-style cafés. Visitors can still see one important feature of industrial Birmingham: the long Victorian water canals that were used to transport goods around the city and to other parts of the country.

These have also been modernised, and tourists can enjoy a pleasant three-hour boat trip through the city's many waterways.

Die Satzstellung von Adverbien

Seite 90

1. a) We usually go to Italy in August.
   b) There's a party at the youth club next Saturday evening.
   c) My dad was singing loudly in the shower.
   d) They worked hard at school last week.
   e) He always drives very carefully.
   f) The film is set in America during the Civil War.
   g) The supermarket on the corner opens at 8 a.m.
   h) The weather is usually warm in summer.

Seite 91

2. a) He's never been to China.
   b) The little boy cycled slowly down the road.
   c) The train leaves at half past eleven.
   d) Andy lived in England for three years.
   e) We sometimes go out for an Indian meal.
   f) She thanked us politely for all our help.
   g) They're leaving for Paris tomorrow morning.

3. a) The team often wins important matches.
   b) If we want good seats, we'll have to leave early tomorrow.
   c) I'm going to the cinema tomorrow evening – do you want to come too?
   d) Lucy works in a flower shop in the school holidays.
   e) ✓
   f) The dog ate the meat hungrily in the kitchen.
   g) Claudia had never seen so many homeless people before.
   h) My earliest memory is playing in the garden when I was three.

Seite 92

Fehler-Check

We often stay in a Swiss mountain hut in the Christmas holidays. Last year it snowed heavily every day. It was very cold, and I always looked forward to returning to the hut at the end of the day. We were usually greeted by the sight of the wood fire burning cheerfully in the fireplace. But we arrived at the door of the hut one evening and found it locked. The owner of the hut normally collected wood from the village once a day, but had not gone out that morning because the wind was blowing so strongly. All we could do was stand closely together outside the hut. It was a huge relief when the owner returned in his car 20 minutes later!

Kapitel 6: *Present* und *past participle clauses*

1 a) I saw him smoking a cigarette in the park. Seite 94
b) Dad is sitting on the sofa reading the newspaper.
c) They met chatting on the same online forum.
d) We got lost looking for the new Italian restaurant.
e) I felt bored sitting at home with nothing to do.

2 a) Feeling tired, I decided to stay at home that evening. Seite 95
b) Knowing that Mel can't keep a secret, we didn't tell her about the party.
c) Not having much money, he got a part-time job.
d) Being rich, they can afford expensive holidays.
e) Not wanting to disturb us, he left quietly.
f) Being cold, she turned up the heating.

3

a) + vi)	b) + v)	c) + viii)	d) + ii)
e) + vii)	f) + i)	g) + iii)	h) + iv)

4 a) Having brushed his teeth, Joe went to bed. Seite 96
b) Never having been to New York before, they first went to the Statue of Liberty.
c) Being unemployed, he doesn't have much money.
d) Having lost my key, I couldn't get into my flat.
e) Looking out of the window, she saw a man breaking into her car.
f) Feeling happy, Pat started to whistle cheerfully.

Fehler-Check

Marie was sitting in her room, studying for her exams. Having failed the exams the last time, she needed to do well. Wanting to become a doctor, she had applied to several medical schools. Not having much time for her friends because she was working so hard, she often felt a bit lonely. But she explained: "My dream is to work with sick people, helping them to get well again. And, having decided to make medicine my career, I have to do all I can to make that dream come true. Not going out with my friends every weekend, I can save money, too. There's a long way to go, but, being very determined, I know I can make it!"

L

Lösungen

Kapitel 7: Relativsätze: *defining* oder *non-defining*?

Seite 98

1 a) Cats are animals that like chasing mice.
b) The Internet is a medium that some people consider dangerous.
c) A nurse is someone who takes care of sick people.
d) Australia is a country that has a lot of desert.
e) A stadium is a place where sports are played.
f) A journalist is a person who writes newspaper articles.
g) Coffee is a drink that is popular throughout the world.
h) Vegetarians are people who don't eat meat.

2 a) She's wearing a dress (that) she bought in an online boutique.
b) ✓
c) ✓
d) Look at all these books (that) I have to read for homework!
e) Here are the photos (which) I took in Madrid.
f) Paul is the only person (who) I can talk to about this.
g) ✓
h) ✓
i) Barack Obama is a person (who) many people admire.
j) ✓

Seite 99

3 a) Jack, who is my nephew, started school last week.
b) The pizza, which was delicious, burnt my mouth.
c) Louis, who has moved to Canada now, gave me his bike.
d) This phone, which I got for my birthday, doesn't take very good photos.
e) Mike, who's a journalist, has written a book about surfing.
f) The film, which came out last week, has been a surprising success.
g) Julie's boyfriend, who she only met last week, has asked her to marry him.
h) The house, which was very old, needed a lot of renovation work.

Seite 100

Fehler-Check

Some people would say that Livvy Dolan is the kind of girl who has everything. In the early 1990s, when she was only six, she worked as a model. Then she started acting. Tom O'Neill, who was a well-known director at the time, cast her in his film "Monday to Thursday". But the film which made her really famous was "Stargazer". She played a young girl who escapes her violent father by looking for new stars through her neighbour's telescope. However, Livvy, who was very famous by now, started to drink and take drugs. She was even arrested by a police officer who caught her driving her car along the pavement one evening. A few months later, she crashed the car, which had been a present for her 18th birthday, into a shop window. But Livvy is the kind of person who knows how to fight back. She went into rehab and came out six months later to take up her acting career again.